God's Parable

BOOKS BY FREDERICK HOUK BORSCH
Published by The Westminster Press

God's Parable

The Son of Man in Myth and History
(New Testament Library)

FREDERICK HOUK BORSCH

God's Parable

THE WESTMINSTER PRESS
Philadelphia

Published by The Westminster Press ®
Philadelphia, Pennsylvania

PRINTED IN THE UNITED STATES OF AMERICA

Library of Congress Cataloging in Publication Data

Borsch, Frederick Houk.
  God's parable. Philadelphia, Westminster
Press, 1975
  1. God. 2. Bible—Parables. 3. Jesus Christ.
I. Title.
BT102.B58 1976   231   75-22443
ISBN 0-664-24786-5

Contents

This little book represents a labour of love in many senses, not the least of which is the love that has been shown by the many people who have lent me their hands and hearts in its creation. They are too many to list by name, but my wife Barbara, Esther Davis, Ralph Frey, Janet Elliott and James McClendon must be singled out. Colleagues past and present have been a rich resource to me. As I write this, the theatre of my memory is crowded with students and friends who have shared with me, not only in seeking to find words for these understandings, but in the belief that the task of interpretation – however many its risks – is vital. The book is a labour of love in gratitude to them.

The book is dedicated to Benjamin, Matthew and Stuart, who have already taught me more about love than I shall ever teach them.

The Church Divinity School of the Pacific   *Palm Sunday*
in the Graduate Theological Union   *1975*
Berkeley, California

Foreword

A Christian may journey to many places and meet with other Christians of widely different cultures and life-styles. Or he may *travel* in history encountering through books and works of art the experiences and reflections of men and women from a variety of eras and societies. Even when he remains at home there are usually opportunities in his own city or town to share with Christians representing diverse age groups and denominational and ethnic backgrounds. They will worship and reflect their faith and practice in divergent ways, making use of dissimilar terms and modes of understanding. Varying levels of education and socio-economic circumstances will often profoundly affect the language of their faith: bumper-stickers and anthems, incense and ecstasy. The searching disciple may also read the works of a number of theologians and be struck by the disparity in their means of talking about the phenomenon of Christianity.

There is, however, one mutual feature in the experience of all these Christians. They all share in common a body of sayings, stories and symbols which are the fundamental lore of Christianity. From the Bible – and especially the gospels – Christians of different centuries, classes and backgrounds draw upon the same stock of adventures, prophecies and parables. Wherever one goes and with whomsoever one speaks there is found among Christians this bond and therefore this sense of community: the remembrance of exodus and exile, the words of prophets, the narrative of a child's humble birth, the bread and wine, the cross and broken body, and the experience of the possibility of carrying on Jesus' message and faith even after his death. These sayings and stories – most especially the stories of and about Jesus – form and shape the common character of Christianity wherever it may be found. They function as the models guiding the interpretation of contemporary Christian experience, and helping to foster new awarenesses of the ways God might be perceived as active in the world.

In one sense these stories are simple and direct, speaking intently to our hopes and passions. Yet just because they do direct our attention to many of humanity's most fundamental concerns – because they act for Christians as life-interpreting metaphors and stories – they are often also mysterious and even haunting. They draw us beyond normal ways of seeing and hearing, challenging the imagination and the heart, in order to offer new possibilities of meaning and understanding.

It is the purpose of this book to talk about a number of these stories. We shall attempt to understand aspects of the manner in which they might have been heard and perceived by Jesus' earliest disciples. This effort – demanding enough in itself – will impel us to take on the interrelated task of interpreting for ourselves what these narratives and parables might mean for us today. Inescapably – because of the very nature of the stories – we shall find that our own lives are also being interpreted by them.

Obviously there can be no guarantee of any measure of success in this venture. Nor can this work of interpretation ever cease. We live in a highly pluralistic and changing world which knows a number of ways of viewing our perceptions of reality and of talking about the multiformity of human experience. There is always the realization that any one person can only struggle with history and life as best as he is able and then hope that his interpretative effort will have at least something to say to others.

I

Resurrection

A shaggy tale used by New Testament scholars to poke a little fun at their more sceptical associates begins when several archaeologists working near Jerusalem unearth some human skeletal remains. Upon examination they prove to be the bones of Jesus. Overwhelmed by the burden of such unsettling knowledge, the archaeologists decide to inform the Pope. The Pope, of course, is shocked. What does this mean for the future of the Christian faith?

Before releasing this information to the press and allowing it to be sensationally exposed to the stunned eyes of the faithful, the Holy Father determines to call a council of the world's great theologians to see if they can help him understand and interpret this calamitous event. What is more, because the implications of the news obviously affect all Christians, it seems wise to make this an ecumenical council, one to which theologians of all denominations will be invited. Slowly and painfully his Holiness works his way down the list of theologians, making telephone calls to each of them. All are heard to make the appropriate gasps of dismay, after which they promise to hasten to Rome for the conference.

The last name on the Pope's list is that of a German New Testament scholar with a reputation for being highly sceptical with respect to all manner of historical information about Jesus. The Holy Father debates with himself whether this gentleman should be informed, but finally, in the interests of ecumenicity and because in this case such an already formed attitude of scepticism might actually be of some use, he makes the telephone call. The German critic, instead of being overwhelmed by the news that Jesus' bones had not been resurrected, registers his surprise in a fashion which takes the Pope's own breath away. 'Ach so,' the scholar responds, 'then he did live!'

More serious discussion among New Testament historians actually raises little doubt as to whether the man the gospels call Jesus once lived. Although it was at one time fashionable in certain schools of comparative religion to suggest that Jesus might have been a mythological figure made over into a historical person, almost all scholars now agree that Jesus lived and that he had a distinctive message and an extraordinary influence upon his followers, even if the content of that message and the character of the immediate influence are themselves subject to critical debate.

If 'then he did live', it is logical to conclude that he also died, and there is good reason to agree that he was executed as a criminal, though the motivations for his condemnation are also debated. For all other human figures, however, their story ends at this point, excepting, of course, the possibility of some measure of continuing influence for that which they have done and thought. But it is precisely at this point that Christianity would appear to stake its most significant claim for the uniqueness of Jesus and his mission. In some manner, which cannot really be paralleled in the annals of other extraordinary individuals whose presence has lingered after their deaths, Jesus is said to have been experienced by his disciples as alive again after his death. According to the understanding of these experiences as reported by the evangelists, this life after death had a basis in physical phenomena and revealed Jesus constituted as a conscious, purposive individual once more.

Here probably more than anywhere else in connection with the gospel accounts the hackles of twentieth-century credibility are raised and the growls of scepticism are heard, not only among those who do not call themselves Christians, but even within the ranks of those who perceive themselves seeking after some form of Christian faith. Even in a decade which appears to permit more latitude with regard to that to which men might and might not give credence, the idea of one physically rising from the dead seems strange, if not totally foreign, to the world-view of most contemporary people, whether or not they are able to articulate that scepticism. After all, one can ask, even granting that such a resuscitation was a possibility, what would be the purpose of a physical body once the actuality of the resurrection was established? Would not the body then even prove to be an embarrassment? What *on earth* could be done with it, or, more to the point of the story as presented to us, what above earth would be its later function? One thinks of those early renaissance paintings with the disciples gazing raptly at the dangling, bare feet of Jesus just at the moment he is drawn through a cloud upwards to heaven. This description points in the very direction of our difficulty, for we can no longer literally conceive of 'above the earth' as a place to go except in a space ship. 'The sacred canopy' which most humans once thought to overarch their world and to be the divider between man's reality and God's has been removed without revealing anything beyond it but unimaginable space. It may now even seem comical to try to think of Jesus' body clothed in flowing robes passing through the troposphere, stratosphere and ionosphere on beyond the moon towards some distant corner of the universe.

We, of course, are not the first to have such difficulties. Nor can we be sure how literally such picture language was intended from the start, but barely two decades after Jesus' death we find Paul attempting to devise another way of expressing the essential idea. He was forced to recognize that many of the converts in the new Corinthian church regarded the Jewish understanding of life after death as absurd if not grotesque. They saw no reason for thinking that a physical body must be viewed as a necessary basis for conscious life. They could, however, conceive of a life of the mind and spirit which continued in some fashion after the death of the body, though there was a tendency in their thought to understand this life as then losing its distinctiveness and melting back into the divine consciousness. In terms of analogy, therefore, Paul interpreted to them the possibility of a new life after death, the means for which would be a new kind of body. 'Flesh and blood cannot inherit the kingdom of God', but the essential person could be, as it were, reborn – a different kind of life being given a different basis for life. In this manner Paul felt that the fundamental understanding of resurrection was retained while yet given a distinctive language and frame of thought. It thus became possible for at least some Christians to think of their own and Jesus' 'going up into heaven' in terms other than those of a flesh and blood ascension.

This process – through which the ideas of one cultural view of life are transposed into the modes of perception of a different culture – always runs the danger of altering the original under-standings so radically as to empty them of their true character. Almost from the beginning Christian evangelists were faced with the imperative either to venture with new thought-forms or to risk the possibility that others would be unable to understand and share their faith. Their answer to this challenge, representing one of the most intricate feats of interpretation in human history, is manifest on the pages of the New Testament. Though often done with little conscious forethought and under pressures immediately demanding upon the preacher or writer, many aspects of the message of and about Jesus were translated from the language and thought-forms of a semitic people into the frequently distinctive anthropological and cosmological categories of the Hellenistic culture.

It is, then, the apostle Paul himself who impels examination of the experiences the other disciples claimed to have had of Jesus as a living person shortly after his death. The gospel narratives, although including notes of mystery and indications of trans-formation, tell of tactile as well as visual similarities between the risen body and the one last seen on the cross. They emphasize the physicality of the newly raised body by describing acts of eating. Yet Paul, in the same discussion referred to above, makes no mention of the story of the empty tomb and, in his enumeration of resurrection appearances by Jesus, appears to include on an equal plane with those of the other disciples one to himself which must have taken place several years after the crucifixion. Scholars have surmised either that Paul did not know of the empty tomb story (was it a later legend given credence to emphasize the physical nature of the appearances?) or that he purposefully avoided such a tale. In writing to a Hellenistic audience, who much preferred to think of life after death (when they did so) as an existence of the 'soul' apart from the body, Paul would shrewdly omit such literal, physical implications. In either eventuality might not Paul's non-use of the empty tomb story, together with his comparison of Jesus' later appearance to himself with those to the earlier disciples, indicate a more subjective and less physical understanding of the resurrection? And, in this light, could not the gospels' descriptions now be understood as ways of insisting by means of picture language upon the intensity of the spiritual experience of Jesus as still living?

Perhaps it is then possible for those seeking to be twentieth-century disciples to believe in the resurrection as an event of the spiritual world alone without violating the intent of the New Testament. The resurrection could be viewed as a happening which affected the inner reality of men's experience but not the common phenomenological world of every man. In such a fashion we might come to think that we had solved the Pope's dilemma in our earlier story: one could come across the bones of Jesus and still believe in the resurrection.

Doubtless there are many who, whatever their own belief, will wonder if this manner of explanation does not all too easily out-flank the scandalous and mysterious character of the gospels' descriptions of the resurrection, so never really coming to grips with the most vital issues involved. However fully we may have been imbued with the Greek idea that man is essentially a mind or soul who has a body and who might then be thought capable of some disembodied existence after death, does not the more Jewish or semitic anthropology actually make greater sense to us? Most of the Jewish people of Jesus' time regarded a human being as a body which had the capacity to imagine, think and reflect. It was conceivable that there might be a living body without these thought capabilities, but there could be no thought without a physical instrument for it. At least this would be true in the only world which these men had experienced and, thus, the only world with which they could meaningfully relate. In these terms one could come to regard it at least as fitting, if not absolutely necessary, that God should have caused something startling to happen in the common experiential world of physical history in order to help the disciples come to the awareness that, through divine power, Jesus' life had proved itself capable of overcoming death.

To this form of argument others would respond that, while it need not be considered illogical to think of God as so bending the natural order of the world, still such an activity is hardly demanded as a basis for belief in the resurrection. The very argument from the infinite nature of God's power would suggest that there were available to him other means for causing the disciples to come to this faith without actually interfering in the general order which was itself dependent on his creative will. What is more, there is danger in the insistence that something had to happen in the objective world in order to occasion belief, for one can then ask whether that which results is really a trust-belief in the Christian sense. It is not rather a form of belief compelled by demonstrable facts in which the will of man plays no part?

No, comes the rejoinder. An empty tomb or even the appearance of a resuscitated body, however amazing or inexplicable in relation to other human experiences, would still have to be interpreted and responded to by faith. It would not necessarily mean anything until individuals came to regard it as an activity of divine purpose affirming Jesus' own message and person.

Indeed, for a generation whose experience involves the reading of science fiction and countless television *miracles*, in which superheroes make dramatic escapes from situations which could bring instant death to any mortal, the resurrection of Jesus could even appear a little tame. All he would have needed to do was atomize himself, shoot forth from the tomb and later rearrange his molecules to reconstitute his physical being. One might even wonder whether men living several hundred years from now will regard physical life after the temporary cessation of all bodily functions as an impossibility. They could come to look upon the story of Jesus' resurrection as a possible first instance of a quirk in the natural order, illustrative of a process which they will have come well to understand. Yet such comprehension might not lead them to the belief that this historical person should thereby be worshipped as representative of divine being.

What the argument for objective, phenomenal events in connection with the resurrection does preserve, however, is the understanding that the belief in Jesus as risen and as God's chosen representative begins with God's initiative and not men's hopes and dreams. Men do not choose Jesus to be of and from God. Only God can do this, to which activity men and women are then to respond.

And yet, might well come the reply from all of us, while this may have been the way it happened for the earliest disciples, what cannot be disputed is the awareness that it does not begin as an objective physical event for subsequent individuals including – most importantly for us – ourselves. Although we can give credence to the historicity of the disciples' *belief* that Jesus rose from the dead, we are left dependent on their faith should we wish ourselves to have a faith based in any way on the physical evidence upon which they claim to base theirs. Yet clearly this would in reality be faith reliant on faith, not upon physical evidence. This awareness is given dramatic illustration when, after Thomas has overcome his doubts by touching the wounds of the resurrected body, the risen Lord says: 'Thomas, because you have seen me, you have believed. Blessed are those who have not seen and yet believe.' Such an observation does not, however, solve our problem; it only gives expression to it. We are forced to realize that the events described in the gospels and by Paul as occasioning the earliest belief in the resurrection do not represent hard historical data for us. This is true not only because we are given relatively skimpy and sometimes strikingly different if not contradictory accounts in the resurrection narratives. It also is true because modern historical criticism is compelled to treat wholly unique events such as living appearances of a once-dead body as beyond the limits of direct historical enquiry.

First let us deal with the apparent contradictions. Reading the stories with care, we find differences having to do with such matters as the time of the discovery of the resurrection (while it was still dark, at dawn, or shortly thereafter), the number and names of the women who discovered the empty tomb, the number of angelic figures present, and when and how the great stone covering the tomb was rolled away. A more serious divergence is suggested when we notice that two of the gospels either describe or point to resurrection appearances in Galilee, while a third tells only of quite diverse visitations in and about Jerusalem. The fourth gospel (though later editorial additions may lie behind this) knows of traditions narrating appearances both in Galilee and Jerusalem. Also of significance is the already noted absence of any reference to the empty tomb by Paul (whose report precedes any of those in the final versions of the gospels by nearly a generation), while the evangelists all set great store by the disappearance of the body from the grave.

One of the greater mysteries of gospel studies is provided by the fact that Mark in his narrative actually reports no appearances at all, but instead stresses the empty tomb and then points to an appearance of the risen Jesus that is to take place in Galilee. This seemingly strange factor is to be coupled with the apparently awkward ending of his gospel both in dramatic and psychological terms. The narrative concludes with the women fleeing from the tomb in terror and, in their fright, telling no one what had happened. This odd conclusion to a gospel has led some scholars to suggest that Mark's original manuscript may have been torn or a final section lost at this juncture. More probable, however, is the interpretation which holds that the evangelist has his own dramatic and theological reasons for ending the story in this fashion. He is, on this view, stressing the awareness that human capacities for description are now powerless and overwhelmed by the awesomeness of what has taken place. The story can only close on a note of fear and amazement in the presence of that which God has accomplished. In lieu of, or perhaps in addition to, this interpretation, one may conclude that Mark merely contents himself with pointing towards Galilee as the locus of the resurrection appearance either to indicate that in this manner Jesus is leading his disciples out from Judaism to preach to Gentiles or to suggest that his final and definitive appearance in glory is yet to take place in that region.

All that the cataloguing of these discrepancies and anomalies does, however, is to impel the critic to the conclusion that the evangelists were generally unconcerned to present anything kindred to that which we would regard as a critical historical account of the resurrection. It is even questionable whether they would have understood that for which we long in our spirit of twentieth-century historical enquiry. While it is not impossible to create reasonable theories which harmonize the major discrepancies (resurrection appearances occurred both in Galilee and Jerusalem, and the individual authors report only those about which their sources of tradition knew; the empty tomb narrative only gained circulation in a limited circle at a later date), such efforts are really at variance with the intent of the evangelists. Their purposes were theological and evangelical. Their intention was to awaken faith, not to impart historical information. They sought to speak to the hearts of men and women – their hopes, faith and aspiration – not just to their reason.

What is more, those who had passed the materials for these narrations on to them had been similarly motivated. Apparently no one in the early Christian communities had regarded it as important or perhaps even possible to attempt to *prove* the historical character of the resurrection by means of some carefully detailed and chronologically precise account of the events taking place early on that first day of the week and in the period following. Even Paul, who at least gives a kind of sequential record of a series of appearances, is, by our standards, blithely inattentive to detail and careful description.

It is also well worth our notice to recognize that none of the New Testament books attempts anything like a description of the resurrection itself. Matthew's gospel comes the nearest to doing so, but even he presents nothing resembling that which we find in later apocryphal accounts, where there are descriptions of Jesus coming forth from the tomb. It is not only apparent that any such activity went unwitnessed, but also that the early Christian narrators recognized that such an action by God could not really be described through human sensitivities. If the explanation for the resurrection is ultimately a cause which stands at least in part beyond history, then, as perhaps Mark most clearly dramatizes, the event begins in dazzling darkness which the human eye could never penetrate.

Even, however, had our accounts been without discrepancy and had they been filled with logical detail, one wonders how much this would assist belief in the resurrection of Jesus in our own time. Even if several of the appearances and the resurrection itself somehow had been recorded on film and then passed down to us to be shown on national television every Easter at six in the morning, there would yet remain a highly significant sense in which such evidence would pose the greatest of problems for historically-minded individuals. The wholly unique character of the event and its suggested cause from dimensions beyond the normal bounds of causality would yet require that the event in and of itself be viewed as *a*historical.

By this we do not mean that the event did not happen. Few historians would be sufficiently presumptuous, especially against the sparse background of the data actually given, to insist that a physical resurrection did not take place, nor for that matter that a supernatural force has never intervened in human history – much less that radically unique and otherwise mysterious and inexplicable events never take place. The point is that historical enquiry and discussion has its limits and its rules. Such investigation presupposes by definition that events of this world take place within an explicable system of causes and effects. Although not all of these can ever be known or adequately understood in a given historical circumstance, it is nevertheless not possible for historians speaking as historians to posit a cause which does not belong to this system. They could not do so and still remain within the bounds of the kind of historical discussion which would be common to other historians. There is no doubt that this manner of limitation raises some fairly acute philosophical and scientific questions. We are not sure what the precise relationship between a so-called cause and an effect might be said to be. Even such a 'law' as that of an effect requiring a determinative cause may only be a statement of the human understanding of universal probabilities. Yet it still remains in broad scope a vital and a necessary rule of historical enquiry. Without it historical discussions would soon turn chaotic and incomprehensible.

What does, on the other hand, present itself to us as reasonable historical information is the disciples' belief that they were having experiences which indicated to them that Jesus was not dead. There is good reason to recognize this faith of theirs and the changes in their lives which resulted from it as events within history which, of course, profoundly affected subsequent history. We must be careful, however, if we are in any sense to rely upon their testimony, also to interpret this information with care. Reasons are sometimes offered as to why individuals should at second hand regard the early disciples' faith as based upon actual physical phenomena which cannot really bear the weight of responsible attempts at understanding. It has, for example, been suggested that the disciples would never have altered their personal lives so radically nor been willing to die for their faith unless they were convinced that Jesus had in fact risen from death. The argument to this point is unobjectionable, but one cannot rightly take the further step of maintaining that therefore he must have been resurrected. There are too many examples in history of men and women being willing to die for all manner of causes, while their views of reality, even when they had the best of intentions, appear upon investigation to have been seriously distorted.

It is far from difficult to imagine scenarios which could account for the intensity of the disciples' new faith and yet offer quite divergent understandings of the cause of that belief. A number of such tableaus have been devised and widely publicized. A recurring favourite involves a clandestine plot. In one version, Jesus is envisaged as the ringleader abetted by an inner band of selected disciples. In other dramatizations Jesus is viewed as an unwilling accomplice in the machinations of his zealous followers. In most of these sketches it is posited that Jesus did not really die. Either his death was faked with the use of drugs or else he was mistakenly taken from the cross before he had actually died and then later revived. In another version his death on the cross was genuine, but certain disciples later spirited the corpse from the tomb and spread the rumour that he had miraculously risen from death.

More than one of these interpretations of the reported events have been composed with considerable ingenuity by minds which may have missed their calling. They might have better made their fortunes as authors of detective novels. At times their versions even sound a certain ring of plausibility, pointing as they do to such factors as the unusually short time Jesus was said to have been on the cross and the pains taken in Matthew's gospel to controvert already extant rumours that Jesus' body may have been stolen by his disciples. Yet the very fact that it is possible to formulate a number of somewhat plausible but quite contradictory scenarios points to the problems involved in such theorization. Because the materials available are sufficiently ambiguous and, as we have seen, more theological and evangelical than evidence-oriented in intent, one can concoct all too many conspiracies. The interstices are sufficiently numerous and varied in character that ingenuity may run riot within them. In addition, many of those who show a fondness for this fashion of intrigue commit in their own way the same errors as do the fundamentalist (or perhaps better, literalist) interpreters who want to insist upon an understanding of resurrection events just exactly as they are said to have happened. In a rather naïve manner, from the point of view of serious historical study, they are prone to make use only of materials which fit well with their theory and to understand these as though they were a kind of stenographic record of what was actually thought and said at the time. The intricacies of narratives which were built up over a period of decades by believing and preaching disciples are rarely included in the perspective.

We need not, however, think only of theories which might seem to compromise the integrity of Jesus and/or his disciples when considering historical processes which could have caused the resurrection belief. One might imagine that some intense and perhaps rather naïve devotion to the memory of Jesus, together with hallucination and even mass hysteria, were the roots of the flowering faith. The story of an appearance by the risen Lord to over five hundred brethren at one time is but one incident which could be subjected to an interpretation along these lines.

One of the more inventive and in some ways amusing hypotheses of this general type suggests a beginning of the new faith in the frightened credulity of the presumably rather gullible women who were present at that pivotal graveside scene. The theory makes imaginative use of certain facets of the Easter morning story. It would seem that several of the women, who were dedicated disciples of Jesus, did indeed come to the grave early on that dawn. Still deep in sorrow and numbed by his death, they intended to perform the last rites⁻ of burial for his body by anointing it with aromatic oils. Not yet knowing how they would remove the great stone which had been used to cover his rock tomb, they were awed to find the stone already rolled back. It is important, after all, for us to remember that these events are described as taking place in the equivalent of a cemetery on what may well have been a misty early morning. Here there were no organ music, lilies, or candles for the celebration of a confirmed faith. The women were alone, and a sense of eerie terror could quite properly have dominated their first reactions.

Suddenly they realized they were not alone. There was a young man standing beside the grave. His appearance amid the wisps of morning fog might well have startled them into thinking him some manner of apparition. He was in fact, however, a gardener or caretaker who had been assigned the task of moving the body to a more convenient nearby place. His actual words are reported fairly enough in the gospel account: 'You are looking for Jesus of Nazareth who was crucified . . . He is not here; look, there is the place where they laid him.' With this the caretaker attempted to direct their attention to the new burial site. But the women were too frightened to take in the true import of the man's words. Instead, just as Mark wrote, 'Then they went out and ran away from the tomb, beside themselves with terror.' Later, however, in recounting their story, and perhaps also in reflecting upon some words of Jesus to the effect that God would not let death defeat his cause, they began to convince themselves and others that God's power had actually revived Jesus' corpse. They and others started to have visions of Jesus based on this belief. So did the faith in the resurrection of Jesus and the beginnings of what was to become the Christian religion commence. It all started with a grotesque mistake and a tale told by some terrified women.

Now, of course, it is not difficult to begin poking holes in such hypotheses. Would not other of the disciples at least have checked their story? We are told that Peter and another disciple soon came running to the tomb to see for themselves. Perhaps there are traces here of later attempts to associate certain of the prominent male disciples with the originating event, but still one would think that men of that time would not readily believe such a tale until they had more evidence than the probably confused tale of these frightened women.

Yet, however difficult it may seem to give historical credibility to this particular theory, or to others which posit some manner of a mistaken interpretation of events on the part of the disciples coupled with later autosuggestion and hallucination, it probably remains easier for most twentieth-century readers of the story to imagine something along these lines than to believe that a thoroughly dead Jesus actually came to life again and physically rose from the dead. The plain fact of the matter is that the character of the accounts is so open to interpretation, and so far removed from any possibility that their veracity could be tested by historical study, that it can hardly be said to be easy now to stake one's understanding of life's purpose and even life itself upon them as conveying historical evidence, much less to go out and ask others to do the same. Wherever else genuinely contemporary and historically minded Christians are to begin, they cannot realistically be expected to win a historical faith merely by wanting to have faith that the gospels present a reasonable facsimile of events which took place so many centuries ago.

Yet those who call themselves Christians obviously cannot be content to leave the issues here. There are other factors in the experience of Christian men and women which require them to probe the inner meaning of this new faith discovered so mysteriously but so vitally by the disciples hard upon the bleak tragedy of the crucifixion. These contemporary Christians have so interacted with the faith-commitment of others that they have at least become sensitive to the possibility that the Jesus of the New Testament accounts might not properly be spoken of as though only a dead figure from the past. Nor are they content merely to speak about him in the manner in which the words and spirits of other great figures are said to live on after them. They are, therefore, concerned to deepen their understanding with regard to that which the early disciples were experiencing and believing in order better to interpret their own experiences and to know if there is a commensurability between what was first believed and what might now be perceived by faith. What, they therefore still must ask, could have caused this new faith and how best can the shape and character of that faith in the lives of the first believers be described?

Anyone seeking to answer such questions can only approach the issues involved with a sense of humility and reverence, for, however one finally inclines in the direction of answers, he must be aware that he is entering upon some form of relationship with other human beings who found themselves personally and poignantly flung into the midst of the most profound of mortal enigmas. Can and do finite beings have any involvement with that which might be imagined as just beyond the boundaries of human understanding? No matter how simplistic the responses of first-century believers to this possibility of mystery may sometimes seem to twentieth-century men and women, and though their words as well as our own may sound as paltry patter when testing such quandaries, few can withhold their sympathy and admiration from the first Christians who found themselves caught in the rip-tide of a faith-conviction which demanded that they try to learn to swim in mysterious seas.

Those who today attempt to hear their words and to interpret them for themselves and others in a responsible historical manner can roughly be regarded as belonging to two schools of approach. There are those who for theological, psychological or other reasons maintain that there must have been some *objective* factors which helped to create the belief in Jesus as risen from the dead. The resurrection, from this general point of view, is to be regarded as an event which created faith and not as a statement of a faith which was already developing in the hearts and minds of the disciples. The resurrection is first and foremost God's affirmation of that which men regarded as weak and of little significance. As such it is requisite that some activity which could only be viewed as a divine intervention in the continuum of objective historical events be understood to be the catalyst for the astounding claim of the first Christians.

The other general form of approach would stress instead the

15

subjective character of the early disciples' experience. Its proponents maintain that the objective data concerning the resurrection not only lie beyond the ken of any legitimate historical enquiry, but in fact are non-essential or conceivably even antithetical to a true resurrection faith. The resurrection belief, from this standpoint, is as much or more the expression of a faith already growing in the hearts of the disciples before the resurrection as it is the result of a new faith born on one particular morning.

The interpreters who continue to argue for objective experience as the basis for the resurrection belief often attempt to score heavily with a theological argument already mentioned. If faith in Jesus as risen and as one who spoke and enacted God's word in a decisive manner remains entirely under the category of what humans come to believe in response to his life and self-offering, then there is run the great risk of finally realizing that belief in the resurrection and in Jesus' divinity is no more than a human invention. In order for Jesus to be known as of and from God, more is necessary than the words and actions of the historical Jesus, which would still remain only the activity of a human being. Men cannot properly create an experience which may legitimately be described as of God. This requires divine intervention in a form which is unmistakable and otherwise unknown to human comprehension. The whole point of the resurrection is that it is God's *yes* to mankind's *no*, his raising up and making alive that which men had declared weak and disposable. Men looked at the cross and saw only failure and an instrument of death. Psychologically and theologically they were incapable of saying any other than that this was the end. It is necessary to posit some extraordinary event which unequivocally indicated to them that another judgment was mandated. In no other way is it possible to step beyond the bounds of maintaining that this was a great man in order to regard his life and death as an activity of God himself.

It may well be admitted that it is impossible for individuals long after the event to participate directly in the objective content of the first Christians' experiences of the resurrection. They can only share in the disciples' interpretations of their physical world perceptions and then seek to find if they are corroborated by faith's experience. Thus it is correct to recognize that all contemporary efforts to believe in the resurrection are rooted in subjective comprehension, but the objective basis for the original belief must be retained as a primary theological tenet and the resurrection viewed, in these terms, as a happening in history, even if now it lies beyond the bounds of historical enquiry. It is also only in this manner that the proper symbolic effects of God's actual participation in the world of flesh and blood experience and his triumph over human mortality can be appreciated.

A somewhat different statement about the objective character of the initial resurrection experiences is made by those interpreters who would stress the *apocalyptic* and *eschatological* nature of belief in the resurrection. Employing these terms (which refer, in the first instance, to the revelations of supramundane meanings, especially as they are suprahistorical and interpret human history from beyond a historical perspective, and, in the second case, to the final meaning and consummation of human experience) scholars of this persuasion would insist on taking seriously the categories of understanding in terms of which the resurrection was first enunciated. Jesus spoke of the end of history as a human enterprise. His words regarding the shaking of the heavens and the darkening of the lights of the skies may be regarded as poetic device in our space age, but they were nevertheless intended to figure the very definite intervention of the divine into human history in an utterly transforming manner. In the light of this transformation, history will be given its ultimate meaning. Whether that intervention is close at hand or distant from us is in this context irrelevant. The point is that it will happen, and the resurrection is to be viewed as the anticipatory beginning of the new age. To interpret the resurrection, therefore, as anything less than an objective historical event is to deny its most fundamental character by abstracting it from an actual historical matrix, and thus at the same time depriving history and its consummation of any possibility of meaning.

Those scholars who would, on the other hand, stress the need for a more subjective interpretation of Jesus' being raised from the dead once again point to our inability to know much of anything in historical terms about the resurrection itself. And, they maintain, even if there had been happenings of a physical and material sort, one cannot proceed in the discussion without taking into account the primary importance of the psychological response to them. The New Testament itself tells us that some doubted in the face of the purportedly objective evidence. For many good reasons, who could castigate them simply on the basis of these visions? As already noted, a dozen other explanations might well leap to most minds before they considered the reality of a resuscitated corpse. And, even should its reality be proven, how might one know whether this was an action of God or just some fantastic vagary in an enigmatic universe or conceivably even the caprice of a malevolent power? In order to believe that it was really God acting after the death of Jesus to contravene the human judgment upon him and the finality of death's interpretation, the response of human faith remains absolutely requisite and must remain the primary focus of attempts to understand what happened to the disciples. The truly decisive questions have to do with the character of that faith and its causes.

In terms of these efforts at understanding, physical events become, therefore, quite secondary. The concentration focuses upon the psychological aspects of the resurrection narratives. One must look for the causes and explanations for inner beliefs and faith commitments. Without positing a basis in external events, can the more than human – some sense of a transcendent reality stronger than death – be regarded as the prime cause of the disciples' faith that the cross was not the end of Jesus' personal story?

Those who would view the matter in this fashion are often content to believe that God does not act in strikingly different ways in different periods of history. It is not important to believe that in 'olden days' God intervened by means of special events but does so no longer. They would maintain that God's real imprint upon human lives is discovered in his activity within the spiritual (or, if one wills, the spiritual-psychological) aspects of their beings. While such activity is not verifiable in terms of sensory proof or measurements, and lies always open to the suggestion that it is but the manifestation of human wish-fulfilment and the like, it none the less has been experienced as a genuine form of reality by many men and women throughout recorded history, though they have interpreted and expressed their experiences in different ways.

It becomes possible on the basis of such an approach to give credence to the reality of the resurrection faith while yet questioning the actuality of the physical descriptions presented in the New Testament. Some interpreters would focus their attention almost entirely on the new faith and hope which arose in the minds and hearts of the disciples not long after the crucifixion. Easter, they would maintain, is not a particular dateable event, but rather is the arising of this faith whenever it takes place. The resurrection in these terms comprises the faith-commitment of men and women who continue to trust in God by perceiving that which was really manifested at the crucifixion of Jesus. While some continue to look upon the cross and to say, in effect, 'what you see is what you get', disciples come to perceive that, through the crucifixion, God was revealing much more to persons capable of faith. When one comes to believe that God's purpose of love shown forth in Jesus is stronger even than death, and that the cross is not the end of the story but that it can create hope and a sense of divine sharing and caring in human hearts, then it is Easter.

This interpretation is, as we have seen, criticized for leaving the understanding of the resurrection too much in the hands of subjectivism as though it were primarily a work of men's faith rather than of God. Critiques are also presented on the basis that this concentration on the meaning of the cross establishes too little relation between the offering on the cross and the person and message of Jesus himself as the one who was crucified. Perhaps it is a caricature to say that he becomes a human cipher whose actual person is of little importance beyond that of the self-offering, but such a seeming devaluation of him as a full participant in history is seen as a danger by many critics.

They, in their turn, would seek to sift the reminiscences about Jesus to uncover a connection between the disciples' experience of Jesus as a person and their later faith that his crucifixion was but the means for a still profounder influence upon their lives. These scholars are sufficiently optimistic in their study of the New Testament materials as to believe that characteristic attitudes and actions concerning Jesus' approach to life can be traced through the disciples' memories and subsequent behaviour. They would emphasize the relationship that Jesus was remembered to have had with God described in terms of the analogy of a son to a father. They would also stress Jesus' readiness, acting under the warrant of God's purposes for humankind, to reach out towards all manner of men and women with a surprising, if highly demanding, acceptance of them in their present condition. This understanding of the relationship between God and men was perceived to come to a unique expression in Jesus' own associations with individuals.

This fundamental alteration in the relationship required a new perception of human possibility, especially in terms of a sense of acceptance by God enabling the acceptance and forgiveness of one's fellows and a freedom and hopefulness in dealing with life's frustrations and limitations. This apprehension of possibility and power was so shared by Jesus with his followers that it had created in them experiences of authentic relationship with God in association with him. The character and strength of this was such that Jesus' death could not be regarded as the end either of the association or the possibility in which he had engaged them. Yes, the crucifixion was experienced as a stunning and temporarily shattering blow, but the life of Jesus already had prepared them for a new kind of faith that came alive again soon afterwards and gave them a recognition of his continued presence with them, which they now were to share with others.

These understandings may seem insufficiently to stress the purpose of the cross (why was it necessary except as a further illustration of Jesus' freedom to give of himself?) and make the resurrection more a matter of carrying on a memory and a message than of a divine activity offering assurance and vibrant hope to the disciples. Yet they are taken further by certain scholars who feel impelled to emphasize the ahistorical nature of the very conception of resurrection viewed as renewed life after death. From this perspective the resurrection is to be regarded not as a historical fact, but as one among several interpretations of a historical fact: this fact being that Jesus continued to evoke faith from his disciples even after his death. Just as God had been met in surprising and anticipatory ways through the preaching and stories of Jesus, so now his followers found that God could be met by others as the disciples continued this proclamation in the spirit of Jesus.

Interpreters who view the New Testament materials in this manner claim that it is a mistake to see the very early church beginning from a retrospective belief in Jesus' bodily resurrection. Rather did they begin with the discovery that they could carry forward his anticipatory awareness of new possibility and relationship. More than this, they sensed the Spirit of God directing them to do so, pointing them much more towards the future in mission than towards the past in memory. Later, as a kind of corollary by-product, the conceptualization of Jesus' resurrection from the dead grew in the Christian communities as these early Christians strove to make use of whatever ideas were available in their time to express this amazingly virile apprehension of hope and missionary purpose. But, so it is argued, just as this was from the beginning a venture in faith rather than of certainty in terms of historical or other evidence and was not limited to an interpretation of resurrection from the dead, so must it continue on the basis of a faith-venture rather than knowledge. So, too, may it be interpreted under other categories than those of a resurrected human life. Jesus himself was a prolepsis of the age to come at which time man's anticipatory awareness of God would be consummated. It must be sufficient for now to sense that what first came to expression in Jesus can continue to be expressed and recognized as a motivation for purpose and hope.

We have to this point uncovered a number of difficult historical and theological problems entwined with serious efforts to understand the Christian belief regarding Jesus' resurrection, and we have outlined some of the responses of theologians to these problems, leaving ourselves with much to puzzle and wonder over. In attempting to formulate our own responses we may well be impressed by certain strengths that are basic to differing arguments. Certainly we may appreciate why some historians would

wish to focus all their attention on those aspects of the resurrection faith which alone can be interpreted and spoken about in
historical terms. We may value, too, their vigorous efforts to
present us with understandings of the human side of the story
through which, by an act of historical imagination, our own human
faith might relate to that of the first disciples. On the other hand,
it is not difficult to see valid reasoning behind the insistence that
an event which is to be understood in any sense as of transcendental or more than human meaning must have some com-
ponent which cannot be evaluated solely in finite and historical
terms. Acceptance of such a factor would require, however, that
in some measure the resurrection be regarded as a *transhistorical*
phenomenon. While its cause may be seen to lie partially within
the norms of historical investigation, in part it will extend beyond
them and to this degree reach beyond our powers to speak of it in
historical language.

In our dilemma over how we are to proceed we may find some
help by questioning whether it is necessary to accept the radical
dichotomy implied in several of the above arguments between the
objective and the subjective in human experience. The human
understanding of reality always involves a response of interpretation – the cognitive and the sensory so interthreaded that no
absolute demarcation can be made between them when we speak
of that which is experienced. No matter what takes place it is
only that which is perceived and accepted as having occurred that
is known to an individual. In these terms, since all we can hope to
share with the disciples through historical investigation is something of the character of their response, the precise form of the
transcendental cause to which they felt themselves responding is,
not only unrecoverable, but not of primary significance for us.
What is significant, if one is to regard the resurrection narratives
as having transcendental and transhistorical meaning, is to
recognize that God must have acted through and in these events
in some way. Therefore, precisely what happened is not nearly so
important as that something or some complex of experiences
occurred which stands the chance of being understood as divinely
initiated action. The transhistorical activity may have been a
resuscitated body, but it could also (or in addition to this) have

been events of a different character, some of them perhaps having physical characteristics though still requiring psychological and spiritual interpretation.

As we ponder again the stories of the first disciples' encounters with the risen Jesus, there emerges as one of their most remarkable features the sudden and unexpected character of these meetings. They did not take place on the disciples' terms. Just as Jesus had acted in many unexpected ways during his lifetime, now after his death the reported encounters with him occur in surprising situations and circumstances. With a consistency that is difficult to regard as mere coincidence, we hear of disciples meeting with an apparent stranger: a wayfarer on the road to Emmaus, a beachcomber back on the shores of Lake Galilee, the gardener encountered by Mary Magdalene, the one who came to share a meal with the eleven disciples. We remember, too, that Thomas did not at first believe himself sure that it was Jesus who stood before him. Even in Matthew's gospel we are told that some of his closest followers were not fully certain that it was Jesus they were seeing. Nor was Paul said immediately to have recognized the Jesus with whom he was confronted.

Of the very essence of these experiences there then would seem to have been an ambiguity which resists any clear resolution into objective and subjective aspects. At least the majority of the reported meetings were apparently quite real enough, but it was only towards their conclusion or afterwards that the belief grew that it was Jesus who had been encountered in the person of an apparent stranger. Perhaps there never was absolute certainty, but, nevertheless, 'Did not our hearts burn within us while he talked to us on the road. . . ?' In such contexts we cannot help but remember words said to have been spoken by Jesus before the resurrection: 'As you did it to one of the least of these my brothers, you did it to me.' Somehow now in personal and often mysterious meetings disciples found themselves confronted by the human face of God which they had known in Jesus. In circumstances of human sharing – frequently in the sharing of food – a personal presence was encountered which was strikingly like their knowing of Jesus. Once again they met one who dared to ask for their love and who challenged them with his love and acceptance of them.

Just as Simon the braggart and coward had become a new man through Jesus' forgiveness and loving need of him – and just as Paul was later enabled to begin to become his authentic self by having his bogus righteousness exposed as self-righteousness through his encounter with Jesus, now also other disciples found themselves so met and meeting.

While we may wish to say yet more about the resurrection appearances, certainly this much must never be lost. If we are to take seriously the disciples' experiences as paradigms and parables for our own, then we too must expectantly be surprised to discover the Jesus-person of God when we are investing ourselves in trust and hope with other human beings. Though wondering men may remain astonished and even scandalized by God's insistence – as witnessed to by the New Testament from incarnation to resurrection – on revealing himself through the crucible of shared human lives, that insistence is too fundamental to the biblical testimony to be regarded as of anything less than the utmost significance.

Further to trust in the belief that God has acted and is continuing to act through Jesus' person, contemporary disciples must look for a faith which has two important characteristics in common with that of the early disciples. It will be congruent with the readiness to trust in God created for the disciples by their association with Jesus – an association which they felt able to continue to interpret in terms of a sense of living personal relationship even after his death. Secondly, there should be a corollary awareness that such a risking of trust is supported by a greater reality undergirding all other experiences.

Our problem and opportunity might then be set forth in this fashion: in response to the disciples' claim of a relationship with Jesus after his death, can later generations come to the faith that – despite all the evidence attesting to the awesomeness of evil and the finality of death – there is a force of life which begins to transcend and overcome? Seen in this light the cross continues to raise the most radical of human questions: in the face of mortal futility and finality, can there be an expectation that the basic reality responsible for the formation and continuation of the universe offers the hope that goodness and the power of life will finally outface evil and mortal frustration? As witnesses to war, terrifying natural disasters, disease, starvation and lonely mean-inglessness in much existence, can human beings also be witnesses to a credible belief that these wrongs are part of a universal necessity that will somehow, and finally, be included in a re-valuing purpose? In basic religious terms, can God be trusted?

The disciples gave their answer to this radical form of question-ing both by accepting the crucifixion as a necessity and by affirming it as a way in which God's love had begun to show its triumph. The crucifixion was proof, if men needed it, that suffer-ing and agony were indigenous to existence, but was also indi-cation to them that God himself not only understood this but did not stand aloof from it – that it was, perhaps in a pre-eminent way, part of his own experience. Yet through and by his acceptance of the wretchedness of the cross he was in the process of transforming it, wresting meaning from meaninglessness, using it as a very way of showing love and then seeking to convince Jesus' followers that it was this and not death which was beginning to triumph. Paul expressed the essence of the Christian response forcefully and succinctly when he maintained that 'love never ends'. There is nothing which

> can separate us from this love: neither death nor life; neither angels nor other heavenly rulers or powers; neither the present nor the future; neither the world above nor the world below – there is nothing in all creation that will ever be able to separate us from the love of God which is ours through Jesus Christ our Lord.

With Paul we too are witnesses to and participants in all the natural and human evil in the world. We know the suffering and death both symbolized and enacted by the crucifixion. We can never live apart from the fear that irrational incompleteness – and at last a pointless finitude and chaos – may be the final victors. Yet if, when using the words and deeds of Jesus to point us towards the boundaries of experience, we too feel called forward to make a venture of faith in the power of God's love over death, and, if on that frontier we are encountered by an awareness of presence which seems to transcend our own imaginations and which corresponds to the sense of person engendered by those words and deeds, then – however we may try to express it – a congruency of belief with that of the early disciples would seem to exist. If, despite and because of the cross, Jesus still can so evoke faith that God's concern for humankind can be trusted and that his presence among them continues, then he should not be counted as dead.

2

End Time

Still across the centuries there can be heard the passionate urgency in Jesus' voice. 'Watch!' 'Be on the alert!' 'Behold!' 'Have ears that will hear!' It is yet audible that Jesus believed he could perceive events happening in the world and through his ministry which meant that God was seeking to do something new in his lifetime. 'Repent, for the kingdom of God has drawn near,' was the fundamental statement of that message.

For most English-speaking people the word 'repent' has a backward-looking cast to it, primarily suggesting sorrow for things done wrong. This does not fully catch the meaning of the Greek word *metanoia*, which signifies a changing of the mind. In Jesus' preaching the theme, while not excluding the idea of regret for past wrongdoing, appears to have had a strong future orientation. 'Have a new understanding!' 'Be ready to hope anew!' The hearer is asked to reorient his expectations and his understanding of how he himself should and can live. He is to do this because 'the kingdom of God has drawn near'.

The expression 'kingdom of God' also does not now convey all that Jesus and his contemporaries would have understood by their use of the phrase. To many modern hearers of the gospel the kingdom of God is likely to be dimly perceived as a place of one kind or another, the dominion of God conceived of as a king. This would be regarded as a spiritual domain or a realm belonging to another dimension. Such an understanding is readily encouraged by a synonymous expression, 'the kingdom of heaven', used especially in the gospel according to Matthew. This phrase, however, is merely a form of paraphrase, a way of avoiding, as many Jews would do, the holy word *God*. It was not intended to suggest some kind of Valhalla – a special place distant from the world of mortals.

When one investigates the use of the expression in the Jewish scriptures and literature more contemporary with Jesus, it is found to refer most frequently to the relationship of God to his creation. The word *sovereignty* picks up something of its nuances, but the kingdom connotes more of an activity than an idea or conceptuality. It is God's *ruling*, perceived in the effects of his interaction with the world. Aspects of the dynamism and motive force of Jesus' central proclamation are caught up in Clarence Jordan's translation of the kingdom of God as 'the God Movement'. In past perspective God is seen as the one who formed and fashioned the universe. Now he is the God who sustains and upholds all history and all creation. He is understood to be the God who in the future will vindicate his righteousness and triumph over all which now threatens the world with evil and a return to chaos. The cry *Yahweh malak*, which is found in several of the psalms, can be interpreted to mean 'Yahweh, our God, creates and sustains all things.' In this sense it is a shout of triumph: 'Yahweh rules!' 'Yahweh is king!' Or it can also be understood as a petition: 'Yahweh, be king; make your ruling known.'

We thus are made aware that for the Jewish people reference to God's kingdom more often brought to mind temporal rather than spatial considerations. God has shown his ruling power in the past. Now there is evil and there are signs of weakness in the creation. When will God vindicate his righteous will and cause his justice to reign? When will his ruling become fully known?

As one may imagine, there were a variety of answers to such questions and also various understandings concerning the manner in which God's ruling was and would be known in human history. The theme was broadly conceived and gave room for different and sometimes conflicting aspirations. Seen in retrospect it appears as a vibrant pastiche of ideas, an emblem of hope to which various beliefs might become affixed.

For some it represented the political victory for which they longed. Israel's enemies would be overcome with the aid of God. The borders of the nation would be re-established, as in David's glorious reign, and peace and prosperity would be known throughout the land. Others anticipated a spiritual order in more individualistic terms. There are found maxims like this: 'He who is separated from iniquity receives to himself the kingdom of God.' Any good son of Abraham could begin to realize the sphere of God's ruling power by taking upon himself the yoke of that kingdom. Through prayer to God as the ruler of one's life and especially through obedience to the Torah (God's law or way of life for his people) the individual could know and enter upon God's kingdom. When a sufficient number of the children of Israel turned in this direction, then the ruling power of God would become fully manifested on earth.

Neither of these approaches was found to be satisfactory by groups who wished to stress the radically new character of the coming kingdom. Its advent would not merely represent a this-worldly political triumph, nor would it be but a process of spiritual development. These fervent believers looked instead for a dramatic intervention of divine power. Human history could be broken into in a startling and cataclysmic manner by a God acting from outside its context.

This attitude was necessarily pessimistic about the present trend of human events. Left to itself, its course was irremediable, for otherwise there would be no need of divine intervention. The current socio-political and moral position was consequently often painted in the darkest of colours. No hope was held out. Its evil and chaotic character would mount. Conversely, the great future age would be one of triumph over all wickedness, a new world of justice and perfect harmony. An acute observer of our own times will recognize kindred attitudes which set forward similar programmatic visions regarding the course of history. Now there is only evil; after the revolution there will be only good. The proclaimers of these programmes alternate darkest cynicism with brightest hope.

The impact of such beliefs upon the interpretation of the moral climate, whether of our time or in an earlier age, results in a disjunctive dualism. Those things or persons which will be destroyed when the new age comes are inherently and unrelentingly evil. Those which shall endure and be saved are wholly good, though they most likely suffer from injustice and persecution now. The grey and twilight landscapes on which most people feel their lives must be lived are ridden over roughshod by the dark beast of this pessimism while there is held forth a vision of the resplendent saviour who will wrest the ultimate triumph.

Imagery like this is, of course, suggestive of the mythological language which such dualism often employs to dramatize its beliefs. Regularly it makes use of poetic device, dreams and visions to convey its interpretation of the present moral situation and that which is to take place in the future. Those initiated into the understanding of the symbolic vocabulary regard these visions as a way of intuiting the true meaning of past, present and future events. This is so because their significance cannot be recognized solely by means of human rationality. Behind them lies divine or supramundane purpose which may be alluded to only by language that points beyond itself to an arena which transcends mortal understanding.

Despite the deficiencies and obvious dangers involved in painting the world in such stark colours, the appeals and values of dualistic interpretations must also be recognized. It is a dramatic way of maintaining that there are distinctions between good and evil and that, despite appearances, relativism is not the final judgment on what takes place in the human drama. Moreover, it offers a message of hope for mankind, contending that the ultimate responsibility for assuring the victory of goodness in the creation is God's and not man's. Men have an accountability, but it is limited. The God who caused existence to be is responsible both for the evil and for the good in it. It is this same God who shall at last clarify his purposes in this strangely mixed universe and, in the end, his justice will be seen to be non-negotiable and to have triumphed.

These differing political, spiritual and supernatural-dualistic ways of thinking and talking about the kingdom of God were currents in the Judaism of Jesus' time, mingling though not always flowing in the same direction. As we look back on the records left in the literature of the period they seem on occasion to have formed turbulent and confusing confluences. By definition we may suppose this would have been so, for men who believed in these ways were attempting to deal with the mysteries of how God might be understood to relate to his world and to human history. Jesus, as one of these men, found himself making use of the language of his culture while also seeking to search out their direction and meaning in terms of his own religious experience.

One of his more crucial interpretations is certainly embodied in the insistence that the kingdom of God *has drawn near*. This phrase, however, translates a Greek word, and one cannot be certain that it corresponds in precise nuance to the Aramaic expression which Jesus presumably used. There are, on the other hand, so many congruent features in the early traditions, laying similar emphasis on the *nearingness* of the kingdom, that we can, in this case, infer a reasonable guarantee of a close translation of his thought.

Something of the natural force of the expression can be heard in other statements in the gospels as, 'When he *drew near* to the gate of the city . . .' or, 'See, my betrayer *is at hand*.' Regularly, however, when used with relation to the kingdom, the verb is found in the perfect tense. There is an action that has already taken place which is impacting upon present circumstances; the kingdom has (already) drawn near. It is not only nearing; it has become near. This seemingly is the result of Jesus' own particular stress. The statement becomes a cry of warning and high anticipation: 'Look, the kingdom of God is right upon us!'

Some hold that Jesus meant that the kingdom had already begun in human life, that it already was being *realized* here on earth. Others maintain that, although Jesus saw the signs of its approach, he still thought of the kingdom as just on the edge of the horizon, dawning but still to be realized in the future. Yet other interpreters find truth in both of these views and emphasize the resultant tension. They speak in terms of such images as the 'atmospheric pressure' of the kingdom upon men's lives. The kingdom is already proleptically present in the world; it is known in an anticipatory fashion. For men of faith its signs and even its very character are already to be experienced, though this is only its beginning, not its fullness.

There is much to be said for this last interpretation which holds in tensile relationship the present and future aspects of the kingdom. The manner in which this tension was incorporated into earlier Jewish ideas about the kingdom has already been noticed, and a number of gospel sayings indicate either the present or near-future character of the kingdom, or both at once. Through such pronouncements Jesus' belief and expectation infused a particular and peculiar intensity in the memory of his disciples.

In attempting to convey some of the nuances of this expectancy one searches for analogies. An illustration which might prove helpful has to do with one's attitudes as Christmas draws near. When does Christmas come? In one view the only answer is 25 December. Then the presents are opened and there take place the religious services and family meals. Yet, in another way, people will have been building up to Christmas for weeks, and much of its excitement and spirit will have already spilled over and touched their lives in the days preceding. As the day has drawn near the way people spend their time and even the manner in which they treat one another may have been profoundly altered. With very real effects Christmas is already happening before it has come in all its fullness. Men and women have already begun to live under its influence.

In an effort to create an experience which would suggest other aspects of this pressure to students, I sometimes resort to a rather crude trick. Entering the classroom early in the week, I announce that because of some necessary changes in my plans the examination scheduled for a week on Friday will instead be held this Friday. After the reactions of shock, ensuing recriminations and in some cases near hysteria have begun to subside, I rather lamely explain that this has been a little gambit. Then, with my remarks punctuated by catcalls, I try to make my points. During those moments when it really seemed as though the examination might be but a few days away, *eschatology* (the concern with the meaning of final events) had struck with full force. The significance of my announcement to the students was found not only in what it said about their future but, more importantly, in the questions it made them ask in their present circumstances. 'What kind of a student have I been? What kind of a student am I going to be during the next few days? (Maybe I had better not go to the cinema this evening.)' Directly, nothing had been done to alter their present situation. Yet, by hearing that a future event was much nearer to them than they had previously believed, their attitudes and understanding of their work as students had been changed profoundly. They were already beginning to live under examination conditions.

Used together, these analogies may have added value in that in their complementarity they allude to two of the effects found in Jesus' announcement. Your joy (of Christmas) and your time of testing are now at hand. Present attitudes ought to be significantly reshaped by the awareness of activities so near that in practical effects they have already begun. Priorities must be changed. Do the hearers of the message know what matters most? Are they prepared to seize with joy that which even now is being offered to them? The proclamation 'Repent, the kingdom of God has drawn near' bears within it, as is always true with the Word of God, both grace and judgment at the same moment. Heard in counterpoint are warning and hope, good news and confrontation.

Yet there comes the obvious and unavoidable question. However potent was Jesus' conviction – perhaps shared even more intensely by his disciples after the resurrection – that God was beginning to act in a new and powerful way, were not he and they in historical-temporal terms mistaken? The gospels report him as saying, 'There are some standing here who will not taste death before they see the kingdom of God come with power.' Granting the strength of early Christian faith, must we not, after some eighty generations of men and women have lived and passed away, recognize that a fundamental error lay at the heart of their belief? Are Christians to continue on century after century repeating that 'a thousand years are but a day in the Lord's sight' and trying to make themselves believe that the fullness of the kingdom will make its advent in but another decade or in the succeeding generation? Clearly any such fervency of expectation is difficult to support and, on this way of proceeding, the kingdom begins to recede on the horizon to become a remote and problematic possibility, no matter with

33

what ardour it is repeatedly proclaimed. (It is interesting to observe how many contemporary heralds of the near end of the world are careful to *sell* rather than give away their property in preparation for the cataclysm.) Just as obviously such a distant and unexperienceable kingdom is so at variance with the thrust of the early church's message as to call fully into question any legitimacy of making a comparison between it and the expectations of Jesus and his disciples.

Our generation is, of course, not the first to become aware of the problem. Even in the period during which the New Testament was written we see the evangelists and others attempting to shape answers to the dilemma. Their major efforts towards a solution suggest that in the resurrection and new lordship of Jesus the coming kingdom has already manifested its power, though the glory of the kingdom in its totality is yet to be revealed. The fourth gospel especially seems to indicate that, with the presence of the Holy Spirit of the risen Jesus among the disciples, the new age has vigorously begun. In this manner the New Testament retains the *already–not yet* tension of Jesus' proclamation concerning the kingdom, but moves forward the understanding of its impact to an advanced stage of significance and experience.

While for the believer there are values to be gained from such an interpretation, we may do better to try to rediscover for ourselves the experiential connotations of that which Jesus perceived to be taking place in human circumstances and in men's relationship with God's activity. Already we have indicated that the unique thrust of his message seems to have been felt in the implications of the belief that God was accomplishing a new alliance with his world in this age. The power of his ruling was even now on the way and calling men to adventure in present situations. By way of contrast we may observe that some of Jesus' contemporaries wished to stress the mighty deeds of God in Israelite history as his chief acts for the salvation of his people. They were for the most part content to live with these memories as the signs of God's favour. Theirs was a kind of religion of nostalgia. In sociological terms many of these people could be styled as supporters of the *status quo*. More likely than not they felt themselves to have some security and a reasonable stake in the economic and politico-religious social circumstances. Their opposites, so to speak, were the men who looked for salvation and a dramatic turn of events in the future. Also viewed sociologically these individuals probably did not see themselves as benefiting under present conditions and so pinned their hopes on a reversal of affairs. It is not meant that either of these groups was motivated by no other than socio-economic interests or that they were lacking in genuine religious concerns, but rather to indicate the general direction towards which they were oriented when looking for signs of God's activity. The gospels present us with good evidence that Jesus disappointed and even angered those who espoused variations on both these points of view.

On the surface of the matter he seems to have been more on the side of those who longed for a future kingdom, and it would be a mistake not to recognize how much he had in common with them. The message of Jesus cannot legitimately be evacuated of the hope that God's ruling activity would yet become realized in full glory. Where he differed from the futurists was in his insistence that this was already beginning to happen. The kingdom did not await men at some date yet to be determined. It was already invading the human climate, creating new conditions and a new aura of relationship between God and humankind. The atmospheric pressure of God's sovereignty was already present. Those who looked to the past or to the future for their primary under-standings of God's salvation were called to an awareness of what God was doing now. Yes, there was value in remembering what God had accomplished for Israel and in recreating memories of his saving power. But the true meaning of these acts could only be appreciated when enlivened by an awareness of his present pur-poses and activity. Yes, those who lived in expectation of God's future triumph over evil were not mistaken in this hope. Yet their aspirations were devoid of content and took on power only in the realm of mythological dream without the realization that the life of the new age had already begun and was making itself available to human experience. Understandings of God's past and future activities only gained living colour when seen through the lens of present experience. Their relationship was only to be deciphered through the interpretation of what God was accomplishing now.

Salvation was not primarily past; nor was it merely of the future age. The life of the new age was begun. The new time was now.

The paramount challenge to Jesus' hearers lay, however, not merely in the words of his pronouncement, but in the manner in which he experienced and lived his belief. The kingdom of God was not for him a shadowy dream, but a reality. It was already acting as a catastrophe for the standards and values of those who were not directing their attention and efforts to God's purposes of creative justice and new possibilities for relationship with him. The dualism which informed Jesus' teaching, while telling of what would one day be revealed, focused the light of the inbreaking kingdom on that which now was being done. The judgment did not wait, but was at this hour glaring into the greyness of men's relativity, showing up the colourlessness of valueless deeds, and causing truth worth – those activities which led to human growth in the kingdom – to shine with the splendid hues of the creator's artistry. The new age's dawning had begun, and now was the time in which men must decide whether they would live in accordance with God's ruling love or seek to fabricate some pretence of shade under the delusion of which they could feel themselves hidden from life's real purposes.

So the pressure of Jesus' message was not heard and seen so much in what it told of the future but in what it made known of present possibilities. Its warning threnody and its accompanying mysterious tune of joyfulness were marching in. The time scheme which others normally used to speak of the new age's advent was by him wound up so tightly that chronology seemed to take on a new dimensionality. Its face could no longer be read through the eyes of men's usual understanding. Jesus himself often displayed a curious but insistent refusal to speculate with regard to clock or calendar time, as though to underscore his awareness that 'the kingdom of God has come upon you' and 'the kingdom of God is in the midst of you'. Even if its full meaning is not yet known, the power generated by its new field of gravitation has already transformed the landmarks of human history.

In succeeding discussion we shall want to make more meaningful the nature of the new possibility Jesus was experiencing and seeking to communicate. For this present, however, we have been given more than sufficient incentive to search for other categories of understanding through which we might interpret Jesus' basic message. In his own time this was set forth as a faith that God's ruling activity was so imminent as to demand a reorientation of human priorities and men's ways of viewing the God–man relationship. Since his culture and religion approached the question of salvation from a time perspective, Jesus responded in their terms, while yet putting such pressure on that perspective as to cause it to bend in order to accommodate something of the mystery always implicated in the human effort to perceive divine purpose. As, however, the gospels moved forward in calendar time and spread into different cultures the question itself found new forms. This was already happening during the period when the New Testament was yet being written, and we have glimpsed an aspect of this reinterpretation, still, however, within a time-oriented perspective.

Many of the Hellenists to whom Paul and other of the apostles preached posed the question of salvation in a rather different manner. The Jews were inclined to say, 'We live in the *now*. When will salvation come?' Their answer was some form of a *then* response. Hellenists, on the other hand, tended to frame the issue in this fashion: 'We live in the *here*. Where is salvation to be found? Is it to be found *there*, in another realm?' This might be conceived of as another kind of existence, perhaps in a purely spiritual dimension, one where unalloyed forms of ideas and modes of being were to be known. Some saw this as a dimension of existence outside of time, the temporal world being but a transitory reflection of that ideal domain.

Many Western Christians are, in fact, probably far more accustomed to this viewpoint and this way of asking and answering the question concerning salvation than they are with the perspective of Jesus' first disciples. In order to win Gentile converts in the Mediterranean world, evangelists, some of whom were Hellenists themselves, adopted this perspective in their preaching. Though often done without much conscious reflection or planning, the transformation was a remarkable accomplishment. Christianity was enabled to become a world religion rather than

37

remaining a sect tied to one culture's understanding of reality.

To set the matter in simplistic but practical terms one may put one of mankind's most persistently asked religious questions: What happens to the individual at death? For Jewish Christians this was a *when* question, the answer being that he will rise to a new life when the new age comes with its fullness. For Hellenistic Christians, however, the response was more than likely to suggest that at death the individual passed immediately to a new order of life. Those who have been saved already have been transformed to the new life. They are alive now in heaven. Actually both of these answers are to be found in the New Testament itself. Although the *here-to-there* view would easily seem to prevail in popular Christianity today, both ways of approaching the issue are to be heard from Christian pulpits, in part because of their place in the scriptures. One can, not infrequently, hear sermons in which both views are articulated without any apparent sense of conflict.

To some this might seem an intolerable state of affairs for a religion to be in. There have always been voices raised within Christianity contending that the Christian gospel lost its vitality when it translated its time-oriented understanding of the kingdom into the *here–there* perspective. As a result there have been frequent efforts to insist upon the futuristic view of salvation and to argue that it is the only legitimate form of Christian proclamation. After two thousand years of Christian history it has not, however, been easy to maintain or reinstate this view except among rather tightly-knit sectarian movements or during periods of great social crisis. Even these movements often have been so imbued with spatial understandings of salvation that they themselves have presented a patchwork of attitudes.

Probably of more significance for a number of contemporary Christians has been the development of trends in theological understanding which ask that the original frame of reference for Jesus' message be seriously re-examined. Much of the impetus for this renewed emphasis results in one way or another from the tearing away of that 'sacred canopy'. After almost nineteen hundred years of domination in Western Christianity, the Hellenized view of reality has begun to fail. Many contemporary people no longer readily conceive of another realm, a dimension other than that of the space and time inclusive universe, in which an ideal life could be said to have its existence. Difficulty, moreover, is found with understanding how this other reality might relate to our own, especially if it is understood to intrude from time to time into the ongoing natural and historical processes. Thus 'theologies of hope' and 'process theologies' seek in different ways to recapture elements of the *already–not yet* thrust of the earlier Christian form of proclamation. The full development of the kingdom, its powers for salvation perhaps not yet wholly formed, awaits us in the future. In this fashion these theologies also attempt to frame some response to the eternal problem of *theodicy*: how can God be all-powerful and all-good and yet allow the degree of inexplicable evil and suffering which we experience? The answers point in the direction of a God who is himself still in the process of gaining full control – who is still working to elicit a free response to his loving justice from his creation. Salvation will come. It is already begun, but it awaits men in their future.

These recent developments in theology are to be welcomed, if not for their actual content or answers to theological problems, then for the tension and consequent energy that they restore to Christian reflection and living. It may well be that the most vital and dynamic period for Christian belief occurred during those early decades when the Jewish and Hellenistic world views (the *now–then* versus *here–there* view of the salvation drama) were in dialogue and paradoxical conflict. In certain transitional passages in Paul's letters and in a work like the Epistle to the Hebrews they are fully engaged with one another. The realm of salvation is already in complete existence to be discovered by men of spiritual perception. God's ruling power has already commenced but will only fully come in mankind's future.

One important result of this tension was to place tremendous pressure on the Hellenistic perspective. If it was to be adapted to the Christian proclamation, it could not present the divine arena as a wholly transcendent dominion only tangential to human experience. As the kingdom which Jesus presented was now entering into the human condition, so had the heaven of Hellenistic Christianity already to be interacting with present reality. Its Lord could not be a distant sovereign but must be available to the daily lives of his worshippers. As the *then* of Jewish-Christianity was so imminent as already to have begun, so the *there* of Hellenistic Christianity had to be so immanent that believers could already participate and share in it. Only so might there be a genuine translation of the Christian message from the one reality perspective to the other.

To some observers it still might appear that the early Jewish-Christian beliefs were in this wise so transformed as to become essentially different from their original intention. It seems better, however, to recognize that neither the time nor the ideal world orientations are anything more than human attempts to think and talk about that which is ultimately a mystery to human understanding. The perceptions of the manner in which transcending meaning might relate to our world of knowing are bound to be elusive and to result in no more than approximate forms of expression. One can also realize that at fundamental levels of human conception the time-oriented salvation scheme of Jewish eschatology and apocalyptic is not to be all that sharply distinguished from the more metaphysical orientation of Hellenistic religious philosophy. Eschatology and apocalyptic may be understood to function in Jewish culture as a form of mythological metaphysics. They are not only a way of talking about the future but also a means of alluding to what already is believed to exist, though it will only be revealed in the future. Understood in these terms they are a way of speaking about eternal realities in thought-forms not unrelated to those of a more evidently metaphysical cast.

When belief about ultimate concerns becomes reflective, it is inevitable that it should do so in language which has a basis in types of mythical and metaphorical expression. If God relates to human lives, he by definition does so in ways which cannot be given precise expression. All high religion recognizes this limitation and therefore resorts to language which seeks both to use and to move beyond reason. The philosopher feels for the words of an appropriate mythology or a metaphysic which natural sciences may seem to presuppose. The poet aspires after rightly intuited metaphor and the dialectic of paradoxical uses of language. In our own century the awareness both of the limitations of human language and of the paradox that the meaning of life may, in one guise, await us in time, though from another perspective be sensed as already formed, is perhaps best given expression in the poetry of T. S. Eliot's *Four Quartets*:

The river is within us, the sea is all about us . . .
Here, the intersection of the timeless moment . . .
Never and always . . . we shall not cease from exploration.

One may well share with Eliot a belief that sensitivity to the possibility of life's greater meaning is to be gained when intersecting approaches to religious experience are held in dialogue rather than when one attempts to resolve the tension in the hopes of clarification. Efforts at understanding may be given a better trajectory on angles forced out between the vertical line of *here–there* comprehension and the horizontal *now–then* perspective than by opting for but one or the other of these approaches. Indeed, it is in this direction that one may best come to appreciate the values of related images which are also used in the New Testament. They speak of a transition to a new quality of life which is beginning to be experienced. There is a transformation from one state of being to another which is taking place in the here and the now. A new man is born from the old; a new creation commenced. A freedom from slavery to sin and to death's lack of new possibility are realized in the very context of the strictures of daily life.

The New Testament, because it seeks to express a faith preached to differing cultures, causes its hearers to experience the tensile approximation of these variant but kindred religious hopes. In different books or passages within the several writings the emphasis may fall in one direction and then another. Jesus spoke primarily about the inbreaking nearness of the kingdom: the end and final meaning of life were so imminent as already to affect human faith. The essential experience can, however, be given expression in relation to men's ultimate concerns, the values which interpret and affect all else they do. This is the language of teleology. The advent of the kingdom of God announces that these values and purposes do not wholly transcend human understanding but are now impressing their meaning on human circumstances. The major concern in all these perspectives is with the frontier or boundary where these ends and goals already are becoming part of the human condition.

Within one frame of reference or another the possibility of this boundary experience has been the compelling interest of most religions. Here man's capacity to begin to transcend himself and the immanent aspects of transcendent meaning interface. The tension between the way things are and the way they ought to be or might be is felt acutely. Both pain and joy are known. Judgment is made on the impoverishments and inauthenticities of life as it has been and is, but new hope infiltrates.

In Jesus' experience of this frontier the measure of this infiltration assumes consuming proportions. The kingdom spills over and breaks forth in the form of pre-happenings. Much of the pessimism of Jewish eschatology with regard to the evaluation of the present age is thus removed. The new age is already informing life with its purposes and meaning. From this vantage past and present are not lost but are believed to be continuously given further interpretation at the future boundary.

This mode of understanding time may be likened to the manner in which a symphony is heard. Although it is only from the perspective of the final movement that the entire composition can be appreciated, yet every part of every movement continues to contribute to the whole even as it is given further depth and meaning by fuller comprehension. As one begins to catch the notes of the kingdom's final coda, moments of sudden new hearing are occasioned. Insight's gift discovers passages in fresh relationship to one another – themes now echoing in major keys what had only been heard before in minor ways.

As with the prophets before him, Jesus seems to have had a similar gift of hearing and vision. Moments of startling insight are fashioned by seeming warps or folds in the continuum of time. Events of history are known in new perspective and relationship just as they are themselves interpreted by meanings to which they now seem to point.

Again we recognize the similarities with developments in Hel-

42

lenistic Christian communities. Because of the compressive pressure of the kingdom's coming the transcendent realm beyond time is no longer valued as a distant dimension to which those of a high spiritual nature may be attracted. Here the pessimism of late Greek forms of dualism is also overcome. The arena of men's history is not just a darkling world far distant from the eternal day which transcends it. Rather has God moved through the boundary to shed the promise of new tone and colour on transitory existence. In moments of inspiration all life and history can be glimpsed from that perspective and so find a new inter-relationship.

For the disciples the resurrection meant a further lifting of the horizon. God's ruling is no more a *terra incognita*. The Lord who is to be met at the boundary where human and divine activity inter-relate is no longer unknown. The infiltration of divine presence is appreciated as having a character like Jesus. The hands of the Lord who brings true judgment on the past and present are known to have holes in their palms.

The one-line prayer from Eliot's poem 'Ash Wednesday' is reflective of the mentality fostered at this frontier: 'Teach us to care and not to care.' The purpose and meaning for life which are recognized with the influx of the kingdom are intended to create in Christians an unremitting caring for all that takes place in present circumstances – to cause them to be healers, opponents of injustice and makers of peace. In them is to be engendered the faith that what happens to men in this life is related to the fundamental purpose of creation. Yet they are also to be a careless people, known for a certain persistent mirthfulness even during great adversity, because they believe that it is God who has fashioned the possibilities for both good and evil in history and who takes the ultimate responsibility for them.

It is not that Jesus' disciples are at some times to care and at other times not. Rather are they at the same time and all times deeply and feelingly to care and yet be careless. It is in a significant manner their sense of carelessness which enables them to keep on caring that is to be their gift to the world when others might be overwhelmed into surrendering all hope and concern. In continuous counterpoint the melodies play on: to care and not to care; warning and hope; already, not yet; present, but still to be known. Among the chief commissions of Christian preaching and teaching is that of keeping this counterpoint in balance, correcting when the imminent and immanent become so dominant as to make inaudible the chords which allude to the transcending – correcting again when expectation is paramount and there is too little involvement with the concerns of this life.

So is one also reminded that this kingdom cannot be owned or possessed in some once-for-all manner. Nor can it be guaranteed by correct formularies (the calling out of 'Lord, Lord'), or by structures and organization. The kingdom's essential activity is creative love with its vital signs of acceptance and forgiveness. Love, to be love, must be given and responded to in a manner which will mean that it is continuously renewing and always costing of something in the self. That cost may be more than repaid in the reciprocation, but there is no assurance. The kingdom's offer is a grace and runs the risk of neglect or refusal as that which is insignificant and unimportant. The giver of such a gift also knows the danger that it will be misinterpreted and that there will be an attempt to use it for the aggrandizement of the recipient. But this venturesome character of love cannot be safeguarded. He who would play in love's game must play with heart committed and exposed or he is suddenly but an observer on the sidelines.

It is to this understanding and to this frontier that Jesus' entire ministry is directed. The ultimate purpose of life has now begun to shape the leading edge of the present. Here past, present and future meet in such a way that all their meanings can be held open to new creation. That consummation lies the other side of the kingdom's horizon, but its power and new purpose are already lightening the eastern sky and bringing colour and shape to this day's life.

3
Parable Events

Arrested by the belief that God was even now working to reshape the inner face of reality, Jesus sought for the means to express his faith to others. He could have attempted to expand upon the conviction in propositional language, but such a way of communicating has its limitations. It may seem to avoid engagement with life's intimate character, instructing people about how things are to be understood in general terms without giving them opportunity to discover for themselves how events might feel, taste and smell when enlivened by the spirit of a new wind. The gospels offer every indication that Jesus was a teller of stories, realizing the need for involving others in the very means by which his message was to be conveyed.

A familiar illustration of the way a story can be used to give new perspective to the eyes of the heart is found in the Old Testament. We are told that, while on his roof garden late one afternoon, King David saw a lovely woman bathing. His desire aroused, he enquired and learned that she was the wife of one of his soldiers. Knowing that this man Uriah was off at war fighting their Ammonite enemies, David had the woman Bathsheba brought to him and satisfied his lust with her.

Some weeks later David learned that she had become pregnant. Though as king he might simply have taken Bathsheba away from Uriah, David preferred to attempt to hide his sin. He thus ordered that Uriah be returned from the battlefield. After enquiring about the course of the war, he suggested that he visit his home, with the obvious intention that Uriah would lie with Bathsheba and later come to believe that the child already conceived was his own. Uriah, however, being the original 'straight-arrow' and feeling strongly the bond with his comrades still at battle, refused to take advantage of his leave in this manner. David next invited Uriah to his own supper and encouraged him to drink heavily. Yet so great was Uriah's resolve that he still refused to accept David's offer and return home.

Frustrated in his less sinful method of dealing with the matter, David now found that anger and fear controlled his sensibilities. What if it were to be discovered that he had thus betrayed one of his bravest and most disciplined soldiers while he was risking his life for the protection of king and country? Feeling himself thus trapped, David pulled the shades of his conscience and sent for Joab, the commander of his armies. Joab was ordered deliberately to send Uriah into the forefront of the next battle and then to withdraw support from him. So did Uriah the Hittite die, and David had Bathsheba brought to him to become one of his wives.

But Nathan, a member of the king's court and also a prophet, learned what David had done. Realizing as did Hamlet that 'the play's the thing wherein I'll catch the conscience of the king', he came to David while he was sitting in his capacity as judge and told him the following story. There was a rich man who had many flocks and herds. In the same city there lived a poor man whose only possession was one ewe lamb. He cared for the lamb and she became like a daughter to him. One day, however, the rich man needed to make a dinner for a traveller. Being unwilling to sacrifice one of his own animals for this occasion, he took the poor man's lamb and had it prepared for the meal.

Upon hearing this tale David arose from the seat of judgment strong with a sense of righteous indignation. 'The man who has done this deserves to die.' At the least he must be made to 'restore this lamb fourfold, because he did this thing and because he had no pity'. Though very likely fearing for his life in the royal presence, Nathan looked straight into that fully awakened conscience and said, 'You are that man!' At that moment David saw what he had done and was brought to his knees in repentance. The prophet offered him hope of forgiveness and eventual reconciliation, but also the knowledge that he must live with the moral consequences of his acts. The judgment, however, was essentially that of David himself. In the medium of the story he was brought face to face with himself in a manner that no form of denunciation could have achieved.

Jesus seems often to have responded with a similar method to hostile questions or apparent indifference among those who heard him. As he expressed it, many had ears but were unable to hear. Like David, they had eyes, but could not see the true nature of their lives. Clearly it appears to have been part of Jesus' style as a prophet and a teacher to employ the allusions of parabolic discourse to engage such people in dialogue. Although in the final versions of the gospels the impression sometimes is given that his parables were intended primarily for an inner group of disciples, nonetheless it is still recognizable that the parables were originally the most public kind of address. They were often intended for those who thought they could not agree with Jesus' message. In this sense they were argumentative. Frequently their tone conveys this undercurrent: *If you cannot hear what I mean, let me tell you this story to see if it will help you perceive what I find God to be doing in our present age.* The outside hearer is invited in and asked to come to a fresh understanding of the human situation and himself within it.

So explicitly or implicitly parables often begin, 'Which of you . . . ?' The hearer is asked to play roles within the story, to identify with its characters and to try to imagine what he might perceive from their perspectives and as a result of their experience. Parables are challenges to genuine hearing and true understanding which are framed for the purpose of bringing the participants in the narrative experience to that boundary where the possibility of the kingdom and present actuality interact. The openness of the future gives birth to an otherwise unknown occasion for freedom in the seemingly all too predictable present circumstances. Not everything is dictated by what has been and appears inexorably to be. Unexpected creativity can take place, and the hearers are invited to share in this experience as a way of interpreting and acting upon life's opportunities.

In this manner, the parables are more than edifying stories. Especially in the form of pure parables they are intended to become living experiences which will reshape the expectations of their audience. In the course of the parable something actually happens to the one who has ears which can hear. So it becomes a kind of story happening or narrative event by means of which the hearer is faced towards that horizon where the kingdom has already begun to dawn. The kingdom is not merely spoken of in the parables. It is in part through their telling that it comes to expression – form and content, story and life being inseparable.

Before we can best come to an awareness of how parable events take place, it is necessary to recognize that the gospel stories and analogies grouped into the category of parables actually come in a number of sizes and shapes. As is true with every artistic medium, the form of the story significantly conditions the manner in which the content is used and is to be interpreted. In the gospels we find at least five general types of parables each of which calls for a different style of appreciation. Although the distinctions among them cannot be held to rigidly and some particular parables may share in characteristics of different types, the general nature of these sub-categories should readily become clear and prove of immediate value in interpretation.

There are first those parables which we can best call similes. These are basic analogies in which it is suggested that one thing or event is like another.

> With what can we compare the kingdom of God, or what parable shall we use for it? It is like a grain of mustard seed, which, when sown upon the ground, is the smallest of all the seeds on earth; yet when it is sown it grows up and becomes the greatest of all shrubs . . .

The primary function of the simile is didactic. It intends to teach us in a direct manner, even if it also asks us to come to a new perception or way of understanding which is not easy to comprehend. Here the main purpose of the analogy would seem to suggest that the kingdom of God may first appear small and insignificant to men's eyes. But suddenly and unexpectedly from that beginning there will take shape the full power of the new age.

If similes may be described as a kind of prose language, the metaphor is essentially poetic in nature. The simile tells us that one thing is like another; it suggests qualified similarities: *a* is like *b* in some ways, but, of course, not in others. The metaphor, on the other hand, directly substitutes an image for some other conception or idea. Regularly the means of comparison are left unexpressed, and sometimes we are not even told what the image represents. Metaphorical language requires that we teach ourselves. Meaning is deliberately left open, asking of the reader or hearer that he grope in the direction of an intuition that might be very difficult to state in any propositional manner. Seen in this light the metaphor is more difficult and is intended to be a challenge to understanding.

Salt is good, but if the salt has lost its saltness, how will you season it?

A third form of parable, well-known not only from the gospels but also from secular literature, is the illustrative story. These tales are told to offer to the audience a picture of how things should be. They function by the principle of wider application. They present a situation in which an exemplary moral action is performed and the hearers are explicitly or implicitly instructed to 'go and do thou likewise'. Familiar stories from the gospels of this general character are those of the widow's mite, the Pharisee and the tax-collector, and the good Samaritan. Though these stories may have further implications, their major import instructs in true generosity, humility and caring behaviour. In comparable situations we are to act similarly.

A fourth type of parable, the allegory, can be viewed as a mutually dependent and interlocking set of similes. In this case, however, unless an interpretation is given, we are not told what each image represents or is like, while yet the inter-relationship of them in the story is so structured as to make the several points of reference – themselves also inter-related – quite clear. The figures in the allegory are intended to offer a simple code which the first hearers would have recognized and decoded without difficulty.

Like the simile, then, the function of the allegory is didactic. It sets forth in story form a specific message not to be mistaken by the hearer. Among instances to be found in the New Testament there is one clear example of the form which, at least in part, was probably a creation by the Christian community to help interpret aspects of Jewish history in relation to Christianity.

A man planted a vineyard, and set a hedge around it and dug a pit for the wine press, and built a tower, and let it out to tenants, and went into another country. When the time came, he sent a servant to the tenants, to get from them some of the fruit of the vineyard. And they took him and beat him, and sent him away empty-handed. Again he sent to them another servant, and they wounded him in the head, and treated him shamefully. And he sent another, and him they killed; and so with many others, some they beat and some they killed. He had still one other, a beloved son; finally he sent him to them, saying, 'They will respect my son.' But those tenants said to one another, 'This is the heir; come, let us kill him, and the inheritance will be ours.' And they took him and killed him, and cast him out of the vineyard. What will the owner of the vineyard do? He will come and destroy the tenants and give the vineyard to others.

To a contemporary hearer of this story the import was transparent. The vineyard is Israel, its tenants the Jewish people, and the one who plants and arranges the vineyard is God. God sent his servants, the prophets, who were shamefully treated. Finally he sent his own son, Jesus, whom they killed. The predicted destruction of the tenants foretells the Roman despoliation of Jerusalem and the Jewish nation. The vineyard, the true Israel, has now been passed on to Christians.

We have few problems with the understanding of this particular allegory because its code is not difficult for us to uncover. Problems do arise, however, when – because of gaps in historical information or cultural differences too great for us to bridge – the code no longer is available. Even the best scholars are uncertain as to how, for instance, some of the allegorical language of the Book of Revelation should be interpreted, and there are passages in the gospels over which debate as to the intended meaning continues. We are not the first to confront these puzzles, and in some cases the problematic character of certain passages may even have been increased by attempts at interpretation on the part of the evangelists or their precursors in dealing with the traditions. Already they appear in some instances to have lost the code or the fuller context which might have been the guide for reassembling the code.

It does not appear, however, that this method presents us with any extensive area of critical difficulty in attempting to assess Jesus' teaching, for allegory does not seem to have been a foremost means of his own style of communication. That which causes the greater problems for critical interpretation is what appears to be an assumption on the part of certain transmitters of the traditions that the allegorical method was one of Jesus' favourite means of teaching. They have, as a result, presented more than a few of Jesus' stories in a fashion which suggests that an allegorical interpretation is required. More than this, they sometimes have provided that very interpretation for the purposes of Christian teaching in their own generation. Probably the most familiar example of this process would be the parable of the sower – the story of one who sowed seeds, many of which were eaten, withered or choked off before they could reach fruition. Others of the seeds, however, produced in varying degrees of striking abundance. The accompanying interpretation is fairly obviously the work of the early missionary church, seeking in the light of its faith to come to terms with a particular problem of its own: why is it that the God-given message, passed on by Jesus to his followers, so often fails to bring forth expected fruit? How can this happen and yet that message be the very Word of God whose will it is to save all men?

The interpretation provides an answer. In some cases, Satan, whose agents are represented by birds, immediately takes away the Word before it can germinate. In other circumstances the individuals who hear the Word have no real depth in themselves in which the seed might take root, or else they allow the cares and riches of the world to grow up like thorn weeds and choke off the seedlings. Yet there are instances in which the Word of God takes firm root and bears with rich abundance.

Although there are ways in which this interpretation is more ingenious than in consistent correspondence with the parable, it is by now so familiar to those who have heard it on numerous occasions that no other understanding of the original parable seems possible. One might even suspect that an earlier form of the parable may have been slightly rewritten, the better to correspond to the all important interpretation. Yet there is a good chance that we still may catch sight of the older purpose of the parable, one suggesting, in a fashion congruent with other of Jesus' stories, that the ways of the kingdom are mysterious and unpredictable. The gifts of God are not in the control of men, not even of faithful disciples. He will not be patronized by men's endeavours in his name. Yet, when the power of God does make itself manifest in human life, it does so in a manner which astounds, perhaps even confounds, human expectations with its richness.

When hearing Jesus' stories illustrating this point, which often make use of agricultural imagery since many of their first audience lived in or near agrarian settings, I am reminded of my own frustrating experience as a gardener. I weed, aerate, rake, reseed, water, feed, roll and watch over my lawn, only to be exasperated by meagre results. Then I glance over and see luxuriant, mocking tufts of grass sprouting through every crack in the path. No doubt there are good scientific explanations for this confounding horti-cultural experience, but the point of similar stories on Jesus' lips is to intimate the seemingly mysterious and, by many human standards, perplexing manner in which God's activity is in the world.

I have taken the space to illustrate the fashion in which the allegorical method of interpretation has influenced the gospels in order that we may be clearer about the nature and function of a fifth type of parable. We may style this the pure, or true, parable. While allegories are a type of expanded simile with an essentially didactic function, true parables are more like extended metaphors. They do not offer any immediate means or basis of comparison. This form of parable is especially designed to lure a creative response from the hearer. It does not function by the logic of obvious analogy. Instead of delimiting meaning, the metaphor of such parables is intended to open up the process of discovery. In this sense the parable is kindred to other genuine art forms. The artist's first purpose is to sing a song, paint a picture or tell a story which will intrigue the mind and solicit the imagination of his audience. Then, by a variety of means – through what is unstated as well as what is given – the hearer or viewer is invited to look at new perspectives and relationships.

Sometimes our prosaic reaction is to ask why the poet could not have stated his message in simpler, more direct terms. His answer, of course, would be that, if there were an idea or feeling he could so have communicated, he would have, but that which he wished to express would not so submit to logical articulation. And, if reduced to common terms of parlance in order to attempt straight-forward description, there is a strong chance that its concerns would never be heard at any significant level of the listener's being. 'Tell it to me, but tell it to me slant,' wrote Emily Dickinson. If you attempt to come directly at me with your message, I will not be able to hear you. If you intrigue my mind to follow you on a tangent which approaches meaning from a fresh perspective, then you may cause me to see what I had not seen before. So are the content and the method inextricably interwoven in the artist's vision. What is to be discovered and the process of discovery are inseparable.

So do Jesus' parables begin with familiar scenes and figures with which or whom the hearers of his time could readily identify: fields and banquets, fathers and sons, brothers and co-workers, labourers and owners, masters and slaves. The audience is shown a vineyard or told about the preparations for a festive dinner. The unremitting secularity of the circumstances and details has a significance of its own. It is as if to say that it is in the conditions of everydayness that the kingdom signals itself. The unconditional approaches man through the conditional and the secular, so that the parables are not *religious* in the sense that they apply only to one kind of people and a particular set of circumstances. The context is more often that of the seashore than the synagogue. The common thread of the parables is found in their concern with the everyday material of life. It is here that God confronts men and that they come to know themselves and their brothers and sisters. It is to these realities that they are to be alert,

53

sensing that in and through them the meaning of life is becoming known.

The parables then tell of forgiveness. They ask for preparedness to seize opportunity and communicate the need for decisions made in the here and now. Frequently these parables speak of joy, and sometimes with humour they suddenly cause men to see that the astounding can happen in life. At times they are meant to shock the hearers out of old attitudes and to direct them towards new hope and possibility even while many of the uncertainties of the human condition continue. Several of the parables warn of impending catastrophe which, however, one is then boldly invited to interpret as new opportunity.

In order to accomplish these purposes the familiar details and incidents, which at first allow easy association with the narrative, begin to twist and become distorted as the story proceeds. The process is similar to the creation of forms of painting and sculpture in which certain of the aspects and perspectives are exaggerated in order to require a new style of attention to them and their relationship with the whole. Those who have eyes that really see and ears that really hear suddenly find themselves in the midst of a disturbing experience. There is in the parables a rearrangement or dislocation of the commonly understood which causes certain ideas, like those of forgiveness or a merciful justice, to reach seemingly ridiculous and, in some cases, scandalous proportions. For a transitory moment normal events are shaken and realigned just enough to allow new possibilities to shine through the cracks.

Clearly, then, the parables are intended to offer their hearers the opportunity of boundary experiences. Their inner action takes place at that frontier where present limitations and future possibility – what is and what ought to be – interthread. They are mysterious because that interaction is mysterious. They intimate a way of viewing reality which goes beyond realities – a genuine change of heart or *metanoia*, a new way of seeing life's possibilities. After the hearing of some parables one is reminded of the suggestion of the physicist who wondered if our universe might be not only more mysterious than we imagine, but more mysterious than we can imagine.

Only new ways of perceiving the world could begin to take such an eventuality into account. Indeed, one would have to trust that the meaning at the heart of all life was seeking to disclose itself before such fresh understanding could enter the arena of the possible. As is the case with many other artists, the fashioner of the parable comes to feel that he has received such a gift. In this sense, parables are believed to happen more than they can be said to be created. It is Jesus' theme that just such extraordinary things are actually taking place amid the ordinary affairs of the world. By a kind of alchemy of the Spirit the common and the surprising are suddenly juxtaposed. This gift of association passes beyond insight as the hearer finds attention riveted by a sense of encounter with that which is felt to be of ultimate value. Both exhilaration and discomfort are experienced, for the revelation is in no way fully comprehensible. Rather does it draw one further into itself by a counterpoint of paradox, different truths resounding in a tension only alluding to harmony. In the same movement there is a feeling of finding and becoming lost, of being trapped into meditation. In an important sense each person must make this moment his own, glimpsing that which the parable may say to him about his own past and future as they are disclosed in the transitional present.

True parables, however, have an integrity and a *onceness* about them which makes difficult any easy application to other situations or areas of life. The hearer is required to accept the story for its own sake and to appreciate its characters in their uniqueness before the possibility of a greater understanding can be apprehended. As with other art forms, parables are intended to draw us into their reality before suggesting something to us about our own. They, along with their integral details, mean in themselves before they cause one to allude to some deeper truth. The pure parabolic discourse thus almost studiously defies the didactic cross-referencing to another set of circumstances as is typical of allegory. Also, with a kind of joyful perversity, true parables will not permit any ready application to similar instances as will the illustrative story.

An effective illustration of a parable which defies allegorical

55

interpretation or the application of an illustrative story is the parable of the unjust steward. We are told of a business manager who learns that he is soon to be fired. The owner of the property accuses him of mismanagement and wants a final accounting. At first the man is overwhelmed and can see no future for himself at all. How can he even support himself? 'Should I become a ditch-digger?' he asks. No, he is now too old and not strong enough for that. And he would be too ashamed to become a beggar.

Suddenly there occurs to him a way of easing his predicament and making possible some kind of future means of livelihood. Before he is fired he will ingratiate himself with his master's debtors. One by one he calls them in. To the first he says, 'How much do you owe?' 'One hundred measures of oil,' is the reply. 'Sit down then with your bill and write fifty,' the steward suggests. Another is asked, 'How much, sir, do you owe?' 'One hundred measures of wheat.' The steward tells him, 'Take your bill and write eighty.'

'What is this?' the contemporary hearer might well ask. What kind of behaviour is being advertised, especially when we then hear that 'the master commended the dishonest steward for his prudence'? Were we to attempt a modern parallel, it might seem that a government official about to lose his job should be congratulated for currying favour with the very businesses he is supposed to be regulating on behalf of the people.

Would Jesus condone or even suggest that we emulate such obvious hustling? 'God forbid,' is the reply of the preacher, and with an even greater firmness is this story ruled out of all Sunday School curriculums. It is not to be recommended as an exemplary story, and there seems to be no sensible allegorical interpretation which will deflect attention from the manifest misbehaviour.

It is reasonably clear, however, that the function of this parable causes us to concentrate on the essential attitudinal change which provides the turning point in the story. We first share in the man's dilemma and are asked how we would behave in his situation. But, since manifest dishonesty seems the recommended course of action, we are forcefully directed to focus attention deeper than the surface appearances. There is humour, too, in the voice of the

56

narrator, for the joke would be on us, were we to think only in terms of the external behaviour.

Though parables must be heard and interpreted in the life circumstances of each individual, so that we may not just claim that the story means what we believe it does and no other, the significant concern of this tale seems to involve us with the new hope of the steward. We are to observe his astuteness, his shrewdness and canny preparedness to act boldly and decisively in the face of changing circumstances. But it is above all his very willingness to hope again, a refusal to accept the apparent limitations of the situation, which is the well-spring for his new life. It would not be difficult to recount contemporary parables about rascals we somehow admire if only because they never give up thinking their next trick is going to save the day and make their fortune.

The parable of the dishonest steward is set forth with the intention of confounding those who would live only on the bases of the limitations prescribed by past understandings and ideas. Its outward features deliberately fly in the face of conventional behaviour in order to push us towards understanding that a new kind of hope, an extraordinary hope, may be called for. The story goes on also to confute those who would give up on the present situation and live for some future dream. It maintains that there is cause for expectation in the present circumstances, even when they appear at their bleakest. It may even be their bleakness which creates the need for a new kind of courage. If men cannot hope in the present time, in which they must make their decisions and take their actions, they will never be able to have faith and come to the possibility of newness of life at all.

In order to seize upon present opportunity, however, men must learn first to dispel illusion and see facts as they really are. The steward did not place his trust in a vague belief that his master might somehow relent or that some stroke of good fortune would happen to him. Instead he dealt with the situation as it was, with eyes that really did see and ears that really could hear. On this basis alone was he capable of making use of past knowledge and present perception. Looking at the facts without flinching, he combined them with his hopefulness to begin to build a livelihood for himself. Out of calamity a new life was born.

At this level of meaning – at the depth where hope and despair do battle in the human heart – there is an ineradicable aura of mystery. How and why this hope begins to emerge is not entirely clear. The hearer is not certain in what circumstances in his own life this power of hope might be apprehended. In the last analysis, however, it must be realized that the mysteriousness working inside the parable and in the heart of the hearer is due not to the intentional design of the teller of the parable but to the character of life which the story enacts. The parable in this case is mysterious at its most telling level because the grounds of hope are an enigma. How and why Jesus' disciples looked up again after the cruci- fixion is a mystery. But that people do this – that hope wells up in them after the most incredible disasters – is a truth with which those who would seek to be engaged with life in its fullness must reckon.

Another mysterious aspect of life is dramatized in the parable of the labourers in the vineyard. Once again the hearer is asked to take on himself the various roles – to be the owner of the vineyard, the men who work the full day as well as those who labour but a few hours or less.

At the time of the harvest the owner of a vineyard goes to the market place to hire labourers. At six in the morning he agrees with a group of men on what will be a fair day's wage. (For our purpose we may say that this was the equivalent of about eight pounds in Britain, or twenty-five dollars in America.) Again at nine a.m. he goes to the market place and, finding men without work, hires them and sends them into his vineyard, telling them he will pay them whatever is fair. Once more at noon and again at three in the afternoon, more men are hired from this same market place.

Now our story, which began normally enough, starts to take on twists which are not so readily understood, for once more at five in the evening the master of the vineyard goes through the same hiring process. But now there is only an hour left in the day, and these hired last will barely have opportunity to loosen their muscles before the time for work is over.

Finally it is six p.m. and the end of the working day. The

labourers assemble to receive their wages, and the vineyard owner presents his first major surprise by ordering his steward to begin payment with those who had worked only one hour. We find this strange and try to imagine what would be fair payment for those who have laboured so short a time. Yet, before our minds have worked through the problem of what one-twelfth of the sum might be, the owner tells his steward to pay them – the full day's wage!

This is amazing, both they and we must think. Perhaps it should be regarded as an act of great generosity, but the danger of its implications are obvious. Immediately we notice the open-mouthed surprise of those who have borne the heat and burden of the day. Possibly they are disgusted, too, and are beginning to murmur against the obviously unjust reward these workers of one hour have received for their labours. But then, as we put our-selves in their shoes, a new thought may occur. Even though our wage had already been agreed upon, surely it is only right that we now should receive substantially more. We may begin to rub our hands in anticipation, until our turn to receive wages comes and we too are paid the original sum and no more.

How great is our sense of outrage! Anyone hearing such a story is bound to be scandalized. This is not the way the affairs of the world are supposed to work or can be allowed to work. No one, purported Christian or not, can get away with acting in this fashion for very long. I have retold this story to Christian business-men and their first response is to the effect, 'It may be interesting that Jesus told such a parable, but a man cannot hope to run a business on principles like that.' Even stronger is the reaction from trade union leaders: 'Whether it is found in the Bible or not makes no difference. We'll have nothing like that going on in this union!'

No, this is not the way the world goes about its business, and we have to agree that chaos would result from the introduction of such a principle into the everyday market place. Although the parable may yet have something to say to our behaviour with regard to economic affairs, it is clear that economic principles as such do not form the true focus of the story's concern with life's meaning. The obvious unworkability of the parable is in fact

59

intended to shock us and to shake us loose from some of our regular assumptions regarding what is fair and unfair. At first in anger and then in some bewilderment we are left groping. If the parable is not speaking directly to economic circumstances, what is the thrust of its metaphorical motion? Is there any situation in life in which such extraordinary even-handedness might have validity and make any sense at all?

Again each hearer must in the end interpret the parable for himself and in relation to his own life. Any efforts at explanation by me are bound in some measure to soften the story's full impact and to distort a message that is so involved with its medium that it can never wholly be separated from it. With this awareness in mind, however, it may be possible and not illegitimate to share of one's own encounter with the parable – of the moments when insight suddenly seemed to receive something of the gift of revelation.

Jesus' preferred manner of speaking about the relationship between God and human persons was a personal one. Frequently he referred to the analogy of parents' attitude to their children. Suddenly it came to me that I had experienced, and now was experiencing again from a new perspective, a character of relationship which might also be alluded to in the parable of the labourers in the vineyard. This is the kinship of the family and, more especially, the concern of the good father and mother for their sons and daughters. In the family, too, we find an extra- ordinary even-handedness with respect to the treatment of children. Seeking to be loving and fair, parents try to give equally of the basic necessities of life – not just food, shelter and clothing – but the children's essential needs for love and the knowledge that they are always their children. With these no distinctions are made. To each child full acceptance is given in so complete a way that it can only be equal. In some sense we may be speaking about ideal parenthood, but we do nonetheless recognize this full and unconditional character as of the essence of parental love. Parents do not love their children on the basis of which of them has been with the family the longest, or how much harder one has worked than another, or even with reference to who has been good and who bad. Mothers and fathers may, for one reason or another, respect one child more than another and have a more effective relationship with one than another, but this will not alter the quality of the basic gift of parental love. They are all their children, no matter what.

To my heart the parable of the labourers of the vineyard speaks of this manner of relationship, not only by hinting at a new understanding of the filiation between God and men, but by suggesting from this perspective something of the way in which human beings are to regard one another with respect to their essential value and worth. By worldly standards and even by principles which many regard as basic to ethics and religion this interpretation of the God-to-man and person-to-person relationship will seem radical and even subverting. It has more than once been suggested to me that, whether part of Jesus' message or not, such an understanding is dangerous to the fundamental moral valuation of life. If acceptance and love are offered without regard to merit or deserving, a proper respect for the moral order of the universe will have to be abandoned. And there is no doubt that a part of each one of us responds to this concern. Jesus' statement that the Father 'makes his sun rise on the evil and on the good, and sends rain on the just and unjust', startles many of our moral sensibilities with a shock. Most often this does not correspond to our private picture of God. Certainly, if we were given the task of being God for a day, we should be much more moralistic than this. The well-behaving would, of course, be blessed while the wicked, if not actually punished, would definitely go unblessed. It is, after all, God's job to uphold such standards. The stereotyped message concerning God as Father which often plays in the back of our consciences has all too little to do with his creative acceptance of us as his children. Instead we frequently hear, 'Just wait until your father gets home!'

Yet now a more familiar parable with a similar thrust comes to mind, as though to suggest that the allusions to the mystery of new relationship found in the story of the labourers in the vineyard must be pursued. Integral to the message of the story of the prodigal son is not 'wait until your father gets home' but the understanding that the father wants you home as his own.

Full of a youth's yearning to explore life a son takes his share of the family inheritance and proceeds to squander it. Finding himself destitute in a foreign country at a time of famine, he is driven to take on the work (terrible for a Jewish boy!) of feeding swine. He is, however, paid so little that he is ready to try eating the husks the pigs feed upon.

In his hunger and remorse he remembers the hired servants of his father who had more than enough to eat. With only his pride left to swallow, he begins his journey homeward. After what he has done it is impossible that his father would accept him back as a son. He has lost his birthright and any claim upon his father. His only hope now is to form a legalistic relationship with him. If he promises to work hard, perhaps his father will take him on as one of the hired servants.

Yet let us see the scene for a moment through the eyes of the father. Peering out of his window one morning (as he perhaps unconsciously had been doing for several years) he sees a figure that at first appears to be . . . and then surely is his son. What is the father going to do? It is his boy, whom he feared he might never see again. He runs out of the house and down the road to meet him. It is his boy coming home!

The father embraces and kisses him. The lad is blubbering about how sorry he is and asking if he could become as one of the hired servants. The father is meanwhile giving orders to have his son's best clothes restored to him and for a great party to be prepared in honour of his homecoming. He has his son again!

It is the elder son, off working in the fields as he has been for these many years, who now has trouble in understanding. Hearing the strains of music from the party drifting over the fields and learning of their cause, he is angry and refuses to join in. And does he not have a right to be upset? His father never did anything like this for him. Caught in the competition of sibling rivalry for parental affection this older son at least would ask, if he cannot be shown more love, that his brother would be given definite indications of less love.

Now the father goes out to reason with this elder son. *Of course you are my son too. Everything you have done is appreciated. You are always with me, and all I have is yours. But come in now and rejoice. It is your brother. We thought he was dead but he is alive. He was lost and now is found.*

As with so many of Jesus' parables the story ends before any final resolution is offered. It is perhaps easy to forget that this parable concludes without telling what the elder brother did. Did he go into the house and dance and sing for his brother's return? Did he perhaps only grudgingly shake his hand, so as to escape some of his father's disapproval, and then go to his room to sulk? We are not told, and it is not hard for a part of each of us to stand out there in the field and to go on arguing with the father. *It just is not fair! Hard work and loyalty should have their reward. Well, yes, even if they are receiving their reward, it does not seem like much of a reward if the other brother is going to receive the same despite his behaviour.*

By sharing in the elder brother's anger and indignation, one can begin to gain some sense of why Jesus' stories were often so upsetting, even to his disciples, but especially to members of the religious establishment. Since Jesus is today so often presented as a kind of troubadour with pleasant moral anecdotes to tell, it must be difficult for many people to understand how he got himself killed. Why would they want to do that to that nice man who told those nice stories?

But this story, and a parable like the labourers in the vineyard, are not nice stories if self-esteem is based on the belief that superior moral behaviour has earned a preferred position in the universal scheme of things (an idea which does not have to have a specifically religious basis in order that one cling to it). Jesus' stories seem to suggest some very different way of appreciating the God-to-man relationship and also that of men and women to one another. The rug of self-righteousness is pulled right out from under both Jesus' contemporaries and ourselves. The ensuing pain is not pleasant (so many of our sympathies are with the elder son) and, should the fall be hard enough and self-image seem irremediably threatened, one could well become angry enough to kill.

On the other hand, let us share again with the father's emotions. In an important sense he cannot help himself. It is his own son, whom he has loved from the moment of birth and will always love, who has come home. In this parable Jesus seems daringly to suggest (it may seem blasphemous to some) that God, too, cannot help himself. We are and will always be his sons and daughters. He will always love us no matter what we do.

A fuller measure of the force and thrust of these parables was brought home to me, as has perhaps been true for many others, when I became a parent. When first we learned we were to have a child, I discovered a rather inordinate desire to have a son. A daughter would have been nice, but the wish for a son was so strong that I was ashamed to admit it. I suspect that this was partly due to the fact that I had never had a brother. Somehow a son might make up for that.

When one wants something so intensely, he figures that it probably will not happen. But I was fortunate and Benjamin was born. My whole heart went out to him; I gave him all my love. It was the most natural of a father's acts. I found all my parental affection fashioned on him.

So much was this so that two years later, when my wife was again pregnant, I lay in bed at night wondering, not without pain, how I was to fake the next twenty years. How was I going to be able to hide from the second child the fact that I did not love it as much as the first?

At this time I had not yet learned what would reveal itself to me as one of life's great mysteries. I thought that love was rather like a pie: the more people there were, the smaller the pieces would have to be sliced. I did not yet know that love works by a very different arithmetic. Granting certain physical limitations, it is yet true that the more love one gives away, the more one has to give. The more one opens himself up, the more room there is for a seemingly inexhaustible spring to flow out. One gives and it is given to him to give, 'good measure, pressed down, shaken together and running over'.

But this I did not yet understand as the time for the birth of the second child approached. How would I dissemble my lesser love? Was it possible that I would find I could not love Benjamin as much? And then, seemingly to make matters worse, we had twins.

64

Also then, as most readers will have anticipated, the miracle happened. Here were two more boys, and yet there was more than enough love to go around. Matthew and Stuart were loved completely, with all a father's heart, and Benjamin was loved not a whit the less.

Now let no one come up to me and ask which of my sons I love the most. There is no way I can answer such a question. My love is given to them all equally because completely, unconditionally and irretrievably. There is no means for them to gain any more of what has been fully given. There is no way they can lose that which was and will always be a gift. One son may grow up to be a famous and illustrious man. In addition to my love for him, I may have great respect for him and we may continue an effective relationship as father and son. Another son may grow up to be regarded as a criminal. He may choose to spurn my love so that it has no effect on his life. But still he is my boy. If there is any priority at all, I may in fact try to bend more of my love towards him, feeling that he needs it more. Perhaps this reflects what Jesus meant when he said of his own mission that 'those who are well have no need of a physician, but those who are sick; I came not to call the righteous, but sinners'.

A mother was once foolishly asked which of her children she loved the most. After a moment's reflection she replied, 'I love the one who is sick until he is well. I love the one who is sad until he is glad again.' If there are any priorities in our love as parents, they are of this sort, imposed by limits on our attention as physical beings. This may also tell us something of the reasons for the father's behaviour in the parable of the prodigal and the elder son. We remember that, when the time came, the father left the party and went out to the elder son to speak to him of his concern for him.

Of course, we are only thinking by way of human analogy. These stories are not intended to tell us of our virtues as parents, but rather of the essential character of parental love. None of us shall ever see such love practised perfectly and, therefore, it can serve only as a suggestion for us. Knowing the imperfections of love in this world, we may even be tempted to be critical of the analogy, but over and over again in the gospels Jesus indicates that it is a most significant comparison, perhaps the best we shall know in human terms of what the Father-God's acceptance and love of us is like. With the smile of exaggerated humour Jesus asks, 'What father among you, if his son asks for a fish, will instead of a fish give him a serpent; or if he asks for an egg will give him a scorpion? If you then who are evil, know how to give good gifts to your children, how much more will the heavenly Father give his Holy Spirit to those who ask him?'

Parental love, as with all other genuine love, is at heart a gift. The beloved never need feel that he must earn or deserve this love. To pretend such a claim would begin to turn it into something else from the loved one's point of view. Instead, he is always slightly surprised by it, finding it fresh and marvellous as not something he himself has created. This awareness seems to be implicit in Jesus' insistence that only those who receive the kingdom of God as would a child will be able to enter it. It is the child-like capacity to receive gifts without the pretence of having earned them which makes possible the acceptance of love as love's gift.

Once more we can hear the cautionary word, perhaps not only from others but from within ourselves: if the offer or relationship between God and man has no basis in the deserving of moral behaviour, then surely one does run the risk of upsetting the whole moral order of the universe. If God keeps on loving his children no matter what they do, then one might as well react as did some of Paul's opponents: *well then, let us sin all the more in order to let God show just how very much he loves us.*

When we ask questions and make objections like these, we are coming close to the nub of Jesus' message and beginning to sniff the smell of scandal in the angry reaction with which it was often received. Nothing will make men more upset than the questioning of the moral basis on which their own sense of self-worth and righteousness is founded. Yet this in effect is what Jesus was doing. He was upsetting the moral order of the universe as religiously minded men as well as others commonly understood it. Regularly the divine offer of relationship has been understood to be, 'Be good, and God will love you.' Among other problems this did not work, and later Paul would echo Jesus' new point of view.

The old religious way led only to a self-righteousness rather than to a genuine response of love and made the disastrous mistake of imagining that love was an earned commodity. The old way had to be discarded and a new way accepted. Yet such a relationship is so disruptive of many of our understandings that we still have grave difficulties coming to terms with its newness: 'God loves you; now be good.' As Paul phrases the same essential idea, 'While we were yet sinners Christ died for us.' Men's chief responsibility is to accept their own acceptability and to place their trust in this relationship which was announced and enacted by Jesus.

Jesus told other parables which highlight the surprising manner in which the kingdom presents itself. He relates the story of a man who planned a great banquet only to find that the invited guests excused themselves. This man then ordered his servants to go into the streets and alleys of the town and to bring all kinds of people to his dining hall until it was filled with guests. Those once regarded as insiders suddenly find themselves on the outside looking in, while the former outsiders know the joy of the banquet. Whatever the reactions of those who might have been thought to have first call on the kingdom, God's purpose will make itself known.

Again we notice that the invitation is not based on the merit of the guests, but we are also presented with another factor in love's equation – one alluded to by the question mark left after the elder son's reaction in the parable of the prodigal son. What if the offer of the kingdom – the invitation of supportive and creative accept-ance – is refused? This appears to be a possibility. Perhaps some will not find such even-handed love worth a response. Yet Jesus seems to insist that God's love must find its human echo in order to be heard. When Paul speaks of the need for faith, for a radical trust in God, he also is reminding that love – to be all that it is intended to mean – must be an activity in relationship. Love is not an abstraction but an offering of self to another which requires response in order genuinely to be known as love.

This could be heard as a way of taking back what has been said regarding the equal and unconditional nature of God's acceptance.

If one must respond to God's accepting love or otherwise find that he is separated from the kingdom, does not this say that God's caring for men has its preconditions after all? Men cannot know God's love until they turn and show a willingness to respond with hope and trust.

Properly experienced and perceived, however, the need for men and women to accept love's acceptance does not constitute a precondition with respect to the giving of love. It is instead a condition on love's effectiveness. The measure of willingness to receive and respond to an offer of relationship places controls on the capacity to recognize the character of acceptance and beforehand forgiveness that is offered. Yet God's gift of love remains unconditional. He loves to begin with. 'We love, because he first loves us,' maintains the disciple.

Although individuals often would seem to prefer the old religious method of turning God into a personal benefactor and seeking to become one of his favourites, it appears central to Jesus' perception of God's ways with humankind to insist that his love is different from the imperfect and *ersatz* forms of love often practised by men. Divine acceptance will not play favourites and so seek to dominate the loved one. It will not, in other words, desecrate the relationship by making the quality or quantity of its love conditional and so destroying the opportunity of response so necessary for effective love.

It is the claim of the Christian gospel that in this relationship genuine freedom is to be discovered. In their heart of hearts most men and women would not really wish love to be any other than the gift it must be to be itself. But again there is the paradox: the gift once accepted requests total response. Nothing is required; everything is asked. The parable of two persons falling in love provides the human parallel. Once the offer of love is accepted, all the rest of life is transignified.

The joy and abandon with which such a gift is to be received and responded to are told of in the little parables of the hidden treasure and the pearl of great price. In each case a man comes across something which he recognizes to be of supreme worth. Immediately he sells everything in order to have that which he now prizes above all. Although we may imagine various ways in which these men had prepared themselves to recognize and secure these treasures, the parables are primarily concerned with the heaven-sent opportunity that is experienced. With enthusiasm these men gave up all else, for all else gained its significance only in relationship to that for which they were prepared to offer up everything. 'Seek first his kingdom and his righteousness, and all these things shall be yours as well.'

The gospels still preserve for us a sense of scandal on the part of his followers that Jesus seemed willing also to act in such extravagant ways. He was ready to spend inordinate amounts of time responding to the most unpromising people. We have seen how the parable of the sower might be understood as a way of explaining his own actions and trying to indicate their consonance with the mysterious activities of God, for this sower, too, seems to cast his seeds with all too little economy. For a similar purpose Jesus may have related the story which suggests that a shepherd, having lost one out of his hundred sheep, would leave the ninety-nine and search for the stray. We, who are not acquainted with the care of sheep, could perhaps rather quickly pass over this parable, understanding it as a general illustration of loving concern. In point of fact, however, the action of such a shepherd would be outlandish. If one wished to be literal-minded, he could talk about the stupidity and carelessness involved in leaving the flock to the dangers of predators in order to go off after one stray. But, of course, it is the function of this parable to allude to such extravagance, to shock the hearer with its seeming foolishness and so to convey its message – in this case the uncalculating lengths to which God's love will go, and which Jesus seeks to emulate in his ministry, in order to win the hearts of men.

This Father God, Jesus insists, does not stand apart. Participating through his creatures he seeks to have the way of love triumph, though its path leads through risk and suffering. Its failure causes his grief – sensed by human analogy as his anger. Yet, though by many measurements weaker than other forces known to men and more easily pushed aside, his way of love remains persistent. The Father is unrelenting with his caring and hope. Because this love is of God, Jesus suggests, it will continue when other powers fail and, however seemingly weak, it will win through its extraordinary generosity.

One wonders if there may be a mysterious but significant comparison with the forces which bring about the continuing proliferation and changes of life. Nature and evolution often succeed by what seems to us profligacy. Incredible numbers of galaxies. Millions of sperm for one life. Against all odds flowers grow on a cliff-side because uncountable numbers of seeds were released. Despite our fears that the constant process of new life being born from the fecundity of death and decay represents no more than life continuously chasing its own tail, Jesus' stories might appear to indicate a belief in the value of a similar seeming recklessness when it comes to counting the cost of love. There is no limit that can be set – no way of counting but by the spendthrift arithmetic of love's largesse. Love, like the power of life itself – no matter how often it seems to fail or how great the odds against it – keeps on trying. Its ways – like the way of the cross – seem both fatal and victorious.

Once more we are forced to recognize that God's means of relationship with the world have an aura of enigma for us. We in no sense fully comprehend, for his ways do not by our worldly standards appear wholly rational or economic. (How fully they contrast with the picture of God I was sometimes given in my youth, for he, too, I was brought to believe, must surely carefully roll the tooth-paste tube from the bottom.) Yet the gospels do often suggest that, were we to begin to imitate something of this kind of unconcern, there might then be enough and more for all to share by way of both food for the body and true soul food.

To go towards such an edge of life, however, one must travel light, packing mainly trust in the expectation of finding more and holding on to very little in terms of worldly standards of security. As a person moves forward, one of his main tasks, both for his own sake and that of others, is that of observing carefully, then perceiving, and perhaps beholding. He is not just to repeat the parables of Jesus but to employ the method of parabolic insight as a way of looking more attentively at life's fabric. He is to seek to create in order to find that he has discovered new moments of

70

surprising gracefulness in the offering of love's vulnerability. Such will be more than stories. They too will be the events of parables through which one experiences the mysterious, scandalous ways in which God's activity is in the world, bringing forgiveness and acceptance, judgment and hope – threatening and intimating of new creation.

4
Acts of Power

Yet faith in the kingdom's possibilities appears to face great odds. A pervasive experience of human life is that of doing battle with powers which seem to be largely or completely beyond one's control. Often inexplicably, frequently mysteriously, men and women encounter stubborn trends in society which seriously impair and frustrate efforts to live together in justice and harmony. At times there seems to be no choice. Either we become victims of the evil in society or, in the struggle to avoid such victimization, we find that we can gain a measure of independence from injustice only by profiting from the victimization of others. Of an equally mysterious potency are the forces operating from hidden springs within ourselves, limiting and continuously inhibiting the personal capacity to act for our own good and that of others. 'Why did I do that?', a thoughtful person may well ask at least once a day. 'For I do not the good I want, but the evil I do not want is what I do,' is the way that the apostle Paul expressed his frustration.

The insights of the behavioural and psychological sciences help us towards understanding these inner forces beyond our conscious control. At least in some measure it becomes clearer why this short-circuiting of our better intentions occurs. From earliest childhood there have been implanted all manner of prohibitions against the full exercise of desires for gratification. Often with the best of intentions parents and other adult authority figures issue a stream of *nos* and *do nots* blunting infant curiosity and wants. Given the imperfections of adults, sometimes these preventive

72

measures are accomplished with undue force. Even when done with what is seen by the parent as gentleness, the impression made on the infant can be that of an immense and intractable prohibiting force. The negative commands are issued and enforced by beings ten times as large as the child, and in fact many times stronger and more able to manipulate – this despite those occasions when the exasperated parent may feel the embarrassment of having been outwitted by a three-year-old. Indeed, it is precisely on these occasions that the sternest reprimands may be delivered.

In order to cope with such an environment the infant gradually internalizes a number of these prohibitions. To begin to get along in the adult world, the child learns in part to function as his or her own *parent*, issuing the commands and sometimes even administering self-punishment when these orders are not complied with.

Obviously there is much that is valuable in this learning process. It is a necessary part of maturation, and without it the child could never grow up and exercise its own decisions and fledgling freedom. The programme is, however, laden with imperfections even in the best of homes and schools. From the dwarfed perspective of the child the injunctions from without and within loom enormous in their proportions. Even on into adulthood, at the level at which the child-like impulse in the individual may continue to hear the parental denial, the prohibitions can seem crushing in their authority and consequences. Yet powerful forces, especially during teen-age years, are also driving the individual on towards experiment and trial and error.

A regular effect of such conflict is the establishment of patterns of guilt and anxiety. While the degree of development of such feelings may be lessened by understanding parents, their onset appears inevitable. A kind of warfare is set up resulting in internal forms of conflict and alienation and measures of self-hatred. Strong undercurrents begin to flow, indicating to the individual that he or she is basically motivated by unacceptable behavioural drives such as anger, sexual desire, jealousy and acquisitive intentions. One result is that persons may suspect or come strongly to believe that they themselves are essentially unacceptable people.

73

In order to establish some manner of equilibrium and the capacity to function in society, basic desires and accompanying feelings are often masked or covered over and driven back deep into the psyche. There, however, they may only gather further strength and continue to direct and determine behaviour, but now in ways which are distorted and unrecognizable to the individual who is at once their subject and object. A kind of divided self develops, and a major consequence of the internal struggle is a feeling of continual inhibition and a sense of being cut off from essential sources of life power within oneself. Explicitly or implicitly the individual may come to believe that distorted directives are being issued by forces much larger and stronger than those in control of the conscious self. Within oneself there may seem to exist ogres and demons, pulling the puppet strings with threats or actual inflictions of pain. Only the best kind of self-knowledge may begin to reveal that these frightening figures are actually the deformed shapes of primal drives and internalized authority figures from the past. Yet such knowledge by itself, although often ameliorating, is usually not sufficient to create a healing peace.

In the process of daily living resultant experiences of guilt, anxiety, self-alienation and its companion of loneliness continue. Anger and hatred – even a kind of rage – may be directed at the self, or the self, unable to live with this hostility, may for survival's sake redirect these forces, oftentimes in disguised forms, towards others. From such feelings and activities issue fractured relationships and an awareness of being separated from others and a yet stronger loneliness and sense of futility.

For many persons there is the experience of being in a kind of bondage. They are puzzled and immensely frustrated by their inability to 'do the good I want' instead of enacting the injustice in relationships that they do not want to do. Time and again their good intentions are inhibited or countermanded, leaving them in a cloud of despair. While various adult mechanisms seek to balance or adjudicate the struggles, the battles exact their price. Energy which might have been incorporated into life-enhancing and growth processes for the self and others is drained off in bouts of depression and anger. Many times the effects are a

74

weakening of the self, not only psychically but also physically. We can only suspect the degree to which both mental and physical illnesses are caused by struggles described in these general terms. Certainly all of us experience at least a vague schizophrenia, a sense in which the conscious self feels regularly called upon to play umpire between aspects of self, none of which is necessarily evil, but which nevertheless exhibit their destructive tendencies. Genuine illness can be a consequence of the lack of integration. Even sickness resulting from external causes becomes more difficult to overcome due to a loss of stamina. A desire to escape or deliberately to incapacitate oneself, attempts to opt out from responsibilities or to create patterns of dependency, are well-known manifestations of physical and psychic disorders. In extreme but not uncommon forms the predominant wish becomes that for the final escape of death.

In a significant sense Paul experiences and describes an externalized version along with his internalized account of this human predicament. Not only must his acquisitive, curious and hedonic life-forces fight to win some integration with his conscience, but there are also the prohibitions of the law. The law of his Jewish society, understood as given by God, is the final instructor in what he cannot do and how he is to do what is permitted. It is, as he conceives of it, a kind of 'tutor' constantly with him as he has internalized it but also empowered with the considerable external force of social and religious sanction.

One should not, Paul argues, make the mistake of thinking that the law is therefore bad in and of itself. 'The law is holy, and the commandment is holy and just and good,' he still believes. The intent of the law is for human goodness and for social order. Without it individuals could not function and society could not be. Yet, confounded and confused, this is not the way Paul experiences the effects of the law. The existential results of attempting to live up to the law's expectations are a further dichotomizing of personality and an inhibiting of the energy which could be used to live more constructively. 'The very commandment which promised life proved to be death to me.' It will not let him grow to become his truest self.

Paul traces the root of the problem back to the story of the first human rebellion. Although he understands the narrative concerning Adam and Eve to be historical, he also interprets it as a story about himself, and, in a sense, Everyman. The tendency to rebel was inherent in humanity. The effect of the law, as it was later developed, was to act as a catalyst, a kind of poultice bringing that tendency to an angry, inflamed boil, while yet not in itself capable of curing the underlying disease.

From our more psychologically oriented vantage we may attempt further interpretation, recognizing as Paul seems to do that, despite its apparent results, there is some necessary character to the story of human sin and that, as part of that character, there is implanted the seed for a growth which otherwise could not have occurred. It is in that spirit that an ancient hymn of the Easter liturgy, referring to Adam and Eve's disobedience, is so bold as to begin, 'O blessed iniquity'. With this audacious statement there is set forward a hope that there can be purpose and meaning in the battles within ourselves that we otherwise find so enervating and self-destructive.

Had Adam and Eve remained in that garden of innocence without eating from the tree of the knowledge of good and evil, or were we somehow to remain in the hedonic innocence of childhood, there would be no possibility of further development. The analogy experienced by the parent is strong. There is a fearful desire to withhold from the child situations which will give the experience of evil, even though such encounters will help bring about the complementary recognition of that which is good. Yet the child remains in total dependence unless such opportunity is given. One accepts the necessity of the child's being presented with making his or her own choices while knowing full well the cost involved. (We may imagine how the father of the prodigal son felt as he gave the young man his share of the inheritance.)

Likewise one wants, even while not wanting, the child to begin to rebel against the parent. Only so can the internalized parent – so necessary though so full of destructive and inhibiting powers – become the means by which the child can begin to leave the dependent protection of home's garden. The wise parent passes on the law in some form, hoping for its internalization, while yet recognizing it also to be an inducement to the knowledge of sinning and a catalyst for intramural struggle and psychic damage. No matter how careful, loving and open the parent may be, this process of passing on must continue – cannot help but continue. The hope is that the risks for freedom and growth are somehow worth the costs.

Yet this hope for a higher form of integration, for an Adam and Eve – human beings – who are freer and more truly human than they could be without the knowledge of evil and good, is not sustained with ease. The signs of personal disintegration, of bondage to destructive patterns and of energy not being used for enhancement of life, are great. So often these forces seem to have developed beyond any realistic human regulation, shattering the myth that we are somehow captains of our souls, the true directors of our lives.

If such seems to be the case on the personal level – human lives being subject to interior forces which are often outside the comprehension much less the supervision of the conscious self – how much more can this appear to be the situation on the larger, sociological scale. To what degree may men and women be said to direct the course of their history rather than being marionettes manoeuvred by strings not of their own making? Those now living did not by themselves create the forces of economic and military warfare, sexism and racism which damage and endanger the quality of human life. Yet they find themselves trammelled in their nets and, in their own fear and desire to escape them, pulling them still tighter.

This gloomy view of the human situation and the possibilities for freedom and growth is hardly novel. Though always rippled by an admirable – even indomitable – spirit of human optimism, it is a current of fatalism which one finds running strong in every age and society. From a historian's point of view its strength is particularly noticeable in periods when societies no longer corporately picture themselves as growing and developing. During certain decades of American history, for example, immigrants and pioneers in various fields seemed to gain some feeling of ascendancy over their individual lives and social destiny. As the frontier closed, however, and especially now as the problems as well as

77

benefits of economic growth are perceived and the world seems far more crowded and limited in terms of its resources and capacities as an environment to withstand the demands placed upon it, the current of fatalism is felt strongly again. Astrology and a recourse to the explanation of evil in terms of causation by supermundane powers have returned to vogue. Religious and psychological philosophies which offer escape from the pattern – or at least some capacity to anaesthetize its effects on consciousness – flower in both new and hybrid forms from ancient roots. There is a strong tendency to turn away from social goals and to make private the ideal of human development, even if this effort now is also undercut by the newer psychological and behavioural insights which we have touched upon, for in their arena too there seems no sanctuary, no pivotal position from which one can be certain of having leverage on one's life.

As one result it is probably far easier now to feel in tune with the language of the first century of the Christian era than it would have been for generations immediately preceding our own. In particular there is a renewed interest in and a capacity for understanding stories which involve the gaining of some measure of integration and freedom from forms of bondage by means of the casting out of demons. The exorcism stories of the New Testament are read and pondered on with renewed attention. The careful reader recognizes the depths to which Jesus felt himself involved in personal battle against the power of evil, personified as Satan and demonstrated through the agencies of his minion demons.

During the last century there has been a pronounced inclination, among Christians as well as non-Christians, to regard these miracle stories as the product of ancient superstition and hence to ignore them in any serious discussions concerning higher religion. If this is now seen to be a form of cultural blindness induced by false ideas of superiority, there is among certain groups today an equally superficial tendency directly to import first-century perceptions and understandings and to set them forth as legitimate – however seemingly anomalous – in a vastly different cultural situation. Especially in an age when so much evil seems to be in control of the world, the temptation is strong to revert to earlier forms of mythological explanation. Society and many individual lives are interpreted as being in the thrall of mysterious demonic powers that can only be dealt with through arcane rituals which appear to have an equally mysterious and primitive character. Vogues arise which are all the more attractive because they are so unrelated to dominant ways of viewing reality. They are indeed intended as means of challenging the rigid exclusion of anything which could be regarded as transcending anthropological and psychological understandings – anything which might be alluded to as supernatural. One suspects that a generation which has lost much of its belief in an absolute source for good is now reaching towards belief in a supernatural source of evil in the vague hope that such might also bring with it some inverse support for a renewed belief in God.

Once again, however, it is our task to seek to translate into the language of our own ways of thought the experiences of men and women of a previous age and to test such understandings to see if they can offer us insight into our own circumstances. By this means we may avoid two forms of naivety – the one born of a belief that all previous understandings of experience are inferior to our own or the jarring adoption of a special category of events called *religious* which yet remain unintegrated with all that we otherwise perceive and think. This is not to contend that there are no forces or experiences the causes of which extend beyond our contemporary efforts at understanding, or to which we may be blinded by the limitations of current ways of viewing reality. Yet one could well maintain that there is evil enough in our world which we do experience and need to combat without going searching for more esoteric activities and causes. Mental and physical illnesses, Auschwitz and Vietnam, present contemporary human beings with more than sufficient wrongs with which to deal. While some of their root causes may not be fully known, there is task enough in struggling against the recognizable causes of injustice and human agony. All too often the origins of this evil lie – not outside us – but in the humdrum of everyday fear and cowardice, requiring no need to resort to explanations involving the fantastic or supernatural. Auschwitz and Vietnam were indeed spectacular triumphs of evil, but the true dimensions of their horror are to be found in the brilliance of their bureaucratic scale and organization giving expression to a need – born in the insecurity of those powerless over themselves – to gain unlimited power over the lives of others.

In these terms we may suggest that the essential experiences of evil which Jesus' contemporaries were confronting were also those in which the causes of personal and social illnesses seemed beyond the agencies of human control, however much they operated through these same agencies. In many ways the people of that time felt their lives in bondage to powers which the consciousness could not countermand. These forces they very often personified and conceived of as demons dominating from within and sometimes also determining the broader course of human events. Although we would employ a different language, we may fully empathize with such experiences. In all too many ways they are our own. We, too, feel ourselves severely restricted in our ability to deal with evil both as individuals and as members of societies. While we know full well how much we contribute to life's dehumanization, we also experience the futility of being overwhelmed and undercut by forces at loose in ourselves and in the larger community which we neither intentionally foster nor will to continue. Guilt, anger, fear and loneliness interfere with all too many of our daily activities and attitudes. On the social scale these have accreted and escalated into forms of racial and class injustice and the politics of terror which appal and often stupefy us into despairing surrender, if not compliance.

Jesus, in his cultural situation, dealt with these forces by commanding them to come out and convincing individuals that this had been accomplished and that they had been restored to a new wholeness. Historically speaking, there is little doubt that he was able to help a number of people to recover from physical and emotional illnesses, sometimes in rather spectacular ways. While the numerous miracle stories in the gospels have too often been retold by the early churches with their own interests in mind to permit us to regard any particular one as a straightforward account of a historical event, the likelihood that Jesus was recognized as a healer in his lifetime is strengthened by the several-times repeated accusation that he did such works by the power of the devil, 'by

Beelzebub'. It would seem that even Jesus' enemies were willing to respect his powers. Their method of attacking him was to cast aspersions on his motives and to question the source of his power to heal. They were forced to resort to the weakest form of human argument: unable to deny the good he was doing, they strove to 'poison the well' – to attack him personally. Jesus' response was to maintain that such accusations made no sense. Satan was not interested in making people whole and well. If he were working acts of healing and restoration through Jesus, he would be acting against himself and his reign would be subverted and could not stand. 'But if it is by the Spirit of God that I cast out demons, then the kingdom of God has come upon you.'

These acts of healing, as part of his servant ministry and along with the language events of the parables, were perceived by Jesus as among the means by which the power of the inbreaking kingdom of God was beginning to manifest itself. They were the harbingers indicating that Satan's reign – the triumphs of injustice and pain – could and would be overcome by a healing and restoring strength which was ultimately to be victorious. Through human life – and especially through his ministry – God was working to redeem, that is to give new value and meaning to the sickness and suffering which were at present an inescapable aspect of creation.

Although the early churches and the evangelists understandably focused much of the attention in their retelling of these narratives upon their Lord and the power to heal which he exercised, Jesus himself seems to have been more concerned with sharing his perceptions of the kingdom's new possibilities. When several of John the Baptist's disciples came to ask him once again if he were the one specially designated by God to herald the kingdom, he pointed them not directly to himself but to these events evoking new hope which were taking place. Blind men were regaining their sight; the deaf were hearing again; lame men were walking and those formerly unable to talk had found the ability to speak. While he may have sensed that God was acting mysteriously and especially through him, these activities did not have to be seen as pertaining exclusively to him. Disciples could share in them, for these acts were the anticipations of possibilities which were intended for all humankind. They were events based in and caused by a fresh faith and hope which the impinging kingdom could create in the hearts of men and women.

It was important, therefore, that those who would share this faith with him should also recognize the significance of these exorcisms of demonic forces destructive to human life. They were not in and of themselves to be regarded as signs which would generate faith where no trust in God existed. It is reported that on several occasions Jesus vigorously refused to display his healing art in such a manner as to compel belief in either himself or the powers of the kingdom. The story of his denial of the three temptations to demonstrate his messiahship (by means of supplying immediate needs, dominating in terms of wealth's power or dragooning faith through miraculous activities) is set forth as a way of indicating his awareness of that which the use of power – especially in its highest form of spiritual power – could do to corrupt those who wielded it and their causes.

Restorations of human wholeness and potential were not to be perceived as a form of magic which would coerce trust in God and his rule. The kingdom's powers were not given over to human control in such a way that they could be manipulated and performed on demand as a function of religion. Rather did they manifest themselves as gifts of promise and confirmation of the faith that God's ruling could penetrate the human situation. The signs of the kingdom's inbreaking took place in response to the needs of men and women who came or were brought to Jesus with a hope already born in them that their lives could find wholeness and meaning. On the one hand, no sign would be given to those who demanded in faithless curiosity miracles indicating that faith was now possible. On the other hand, those whose hope had begun to awaken a willingness to trust in God's sovereignty and capacity to redeem were enabled to see the signs of the new age's advent.

That which the disciples seem to have come to regard as extraordinary about Jesus was the manner in which this sacramental power was focused and made effective in his ministry. In many of those who were overwhelmed by demonic forces and had lost much of their capacity to battle for meaning and purpose in their lives, Jesus was able to awaken a new hope and trust. His trust healed their distrust. His faith created a response of faith. Individuals who were physically and/or emotionally ill due to the ravages of guilt, fear and loneliness and who often were rejected by society, found in Jesus one who could offer them a potent gift of new hope and health. A paradigm for this activity is the story of the healing of the paralytic. Jesus' first concern is to convince the man that his sins can be and are forgiven. He offers the paralytic absolution and his own acceptance of him. The healing follows as a result of the man's new strength and purpose for life. As with others touched by Jesus' life the man is then enabled also to 'go home', restored in such a way as to believe that he is acceptable and capable of accepting others in community.

We do not claim that our interpretations are adequate fully to explain Jesus' healing ministry in the terms of our understandings. Although we may witness some healings that are virtually instantaneous, the majority of the restorations to health which we see accomplished or encouraged through renewed hope and faith are progressions which may take days or even months. It may be that the faith which Jesus was able to communicate was too intense for us wholly to comprehend. Nonetheless, Jesus' own attitude would seem to suggest that the power by which these victories over human incapacity are won is not to be regarded as completely foreign to human understanding. Although the kingdom's activities may sometimes be perceived as unusual and startling, they are not therefore to be viewed as radically distinctive from the capacities with which human life is already endowed. The power of God's new reign was working through and not apart from Jesus' human capabilities and those of his disciples. Partly for this reason the earliest traditions tended to avoid the use of language which would stress what might popularly be understood as the *miraculous* aspects of Jesus' activities. The preferred word for describing them was *dunameis* – from which our word *dynamite* is derived. They were little explosions created by the kingdom's impingement, but as acts of power rather than miracles the emphasis fell at least as much on the manner in which they were accomplished through human agency as on other-worldly origin. The power was at once natural and supernatural – a heightening due to the drawing near of the kingdom of that which God had already made inherent in the world.

The gospels indicate that the recognizable manifestations of this power in human lives are acts of forgiveness, acceptance and reconciliation. We are told, for example, a story about how such power touched the life of a rich tax collector by the name of Zacchaeus.

On the day that the prophet from Nazareth entered Zacchaeus' home town of Jericho, there were many who wondered whom he would honour with his presence. Zacchaeus would not have concerned himself with that question. A prophet could not very well associate with a tax-gatherer and retain his purity. The very principle of Zacchaeus' profession required that he be a hard and ruthless man. He made his living by overcharging his fellow Jews and by acting obsequiously to the Roman officials, with the result that he was disliked by his countrymen and held in contempt by the authorities. But he might at least see Jesus and perhaps hear a word that would say something to his condition. Being short in stature and forgetting for the moment any sense of his own dignity, he climbed into a tree to peer over the crowd.

Whether Jesus knew who Zacchaeus was or somehow perceived his condition and the difference that acceptance might make in him, we are not told in the story. But when he came to that place, he looked up and said, 'Hurry down, Zacchaeus, for I must stay in your house today.' People in the crowd, we are told, began to grumble, 'This man has gone as a guest to the house of a sinner.' But Zacchaeus' response to this extraordinary act of acceptance of him personally was immediately to announce plans to make abundant restitution for his acts of fraud and to help the poor.

So was Zacchaeus set free from his own form of bondage. He became more the self he wished to be through the power of Jesus' act of reaching out to him. The acceptance was radical: not glossing over the evil which Zacchaeus had done and so allowing guilt to continue to fester within him, but forgiving and offering both understanding and a challenge to a new life. Zacchaeus was both healed and saved – freed *from* his emotional illness and *for* a new sense of his humanity.

The character of such freedom and one of the ways in which it can also result in healing activities are given expression in the familiar parable of the good Samaritan. The story is told in response to a man seeking to justify a narrowing definition of love. 'Who is my neighbour?' In other words, 'Whom may I *not* treat with costly love? Whose needs may I safely exclude and still keep my conscience intact?' Such are very human questions and, in the exigencies of everyday life and its many demands, cannot lightly be set aside. There is no person who does not make some such enquiry of his conscience on an almost daily basis.

Jesus' response by parable cuts to the heart of the question's intent by telling of a man who did not need a law or definition as a shell of protection. The question is thus not answered at the level of specifics. Only in a generalized sense does the story suggest that all men are brothers. Only in a secondary manner does it respond to the question, 'Am I my brother's keeper?' by prompting, 'You are your brother's brother.' What the story most forcibly does do, however, is to point the one who asked the question back to his own motives. It asks a probing question in return. In comparison with the Samaritan, what is he hung up on in his own life? Could you – would you like to – be free enough to respond to human need wherever you meet it and without feeling compelled to ask how you might limit yourself and still retain a respectful conscience in your own eyes?

It is this concern with the power for liberation and the human capacity for growth which is the heartbeat of the gospel message. The problems perceived have little to do with a lack of knowledge concerning how people are to behave. Jesus appears to have been disinclined to engage in lengthy disputations on ethical topics or to present some special teaching of his own. He even seems rather curt with those who ask him about the way to eternal life. 'You know the commandments,' is his response. The major difficulty is instead perceived as enfeeblement and the short-circuiting of human capabilities. The advent of the kingdom offers the enabling power for a new orientation – a style of life suggested by that of the Samaritan. In responding to God's initiative of love men and women come to know in this relationship that they are lov*able* and now able to love themselves in such a way as to begin to offer love.

In caring for others they make this love known and also find that they are loving the God who indwells all human lives and seeks to come to expression in them. Such love may be expressed in many individual ways, but all are to be characterized by a positive desire to seek out opportunities for caring rather than a defensive and negative interpretation of right actions.

By means of such power the vicious circle of fear and inability to act creatively is begun to be cracked open. So also is the bondage to necessity and to the legalistic attitude towards human relations countermanded. Once again the dawning of the kingdom is seen to lift the horizon of human possibility, and Jesus, as the herald of the kingdom, sets forward in his stories and enacted parables an attitude which challenges all pietism and all safe definitions of *religious* behaviour. He makes it requisite for all who would seek to follow him towards the kingdom's frontier to pass beyond the charted areas of mere ethical morality. They are asked to go forward with him in a direction of adventuresome and risking love.

Not only friends but enemies are to be loved. One is to pray even for persecutors. There is a vital sense in which it is as wrong to call a brother a fool as it is to kill him. By indicating through a kind of hyperbolic inversion that punishment for such a remark might even be greater than that for murder, Jesus presses home the significance of the entire motivation for life as the basis for his followers' behaviour. It is not a sufficient response to the new forgiveness only not to kill. Mere refraining from doing bodily injury to a fellow being – one who also bears the image of God – should be replaced by an abiding concern for the other's welfare. To derogate the other's humanity is to lessen and dehumanize, a tendency which can only be overcome by a new spirit of creative acceptance.

In a similar spirit one is told that an attitude of lustful desire is the worst sexual sin. Lust views another as less than a full sharer in human values and possibilities. Only an awareness of one's own complete acceptance can enable a participation in the full creatureliness of a sister or brother as one of Holy Being's manifestations in the world.

In these and other ways Jesus maintains that the righteousness of his disciples should exceed that of the scribes and Pharisees, for otherwise they will not realize their participation in the power of God's kingdom. This exhortation is not a demand for more scrupulosity with regard to the practice of the law nor is it, as it is sometimes represented, a rejection of the Jewish law. The Pharisees can, in fact, be commended for their observances of the law, involving many acts of sacrifice and charity. The law or Torah can have an important function as a kind of guide for behaviour. Jesus recognizes that individuals and society need and can be aided by such guidance. In his teaching he also realizes that there are many situations where it is necessary to say *no* in order to say *yes* to a higher value or purpose. His point is that the law attitude, viewed as a way of seeking to secure one's own righteousness and practised from a negative standpoint concerned primarily with not committing overt acts of sin, is an insufficient response on the part of those who have begun to trust in the advent of God's ruling. Acceptance into a right relationship with God is a gift that is already offered even (to the Pharisees' dismay) to tax-gatherers and sinners. The response to this acceptance is a new life-style based on a desire for justice and love for others.

'For the whole law is fulfilled in one statement,' maintains Paul. 'You shall love your neighbour as yourself.' To the near neighbour the immediate caring of understanding acceptance is given. To the more distant neighbour this caring is manifested in the form of a living demand for justice, asking that this person be given the same opportunities for the development of human potential as one rightly desires for oneself. Not sinning in any legalistic sense is only as it were a by-product of this orientation. This is the new law of which the prophet has spoken, written on the heart and not on tablets of stone. It is only by its motivation that the disciples may exceed the righteousness of the scribes and Pharisees.

The capstone of Jesus' remarks concerning behaviour in response to the kingdom's inbreaking so stresses the positive orientation of his concern as to seem hyperbolic beyond the point of absurdity. 'You must therefore be perfect just as your heavenly Father is perfect' or, as it is also translated, 'You must therefore be all goodness, just as your heavenly Father is all good.' To this statement there must have been many devout Christians whose first response – perhaps especially in their innermost thoughts – has been to the effect, 'You must be joking!' The greater the individual's growth in commitment to the kingdom the more likely is there to be a sense of impossible distance between his own goodness and that of All Holy Being.

The point of Jesus' remark, however, is once more to direct men and women away from limited definitions of personal morality. Humanity and its possibilities cannot be defined solely on their own terms. As God's special manifestations of consciousness and as creatures intended for responsibility in the creation according to his purposes, the destiny of human beings has no known limitations. No final worldly standard can be set for their development as lovers and creators of their own goodness and that of others. The direction of the Christian ethic points to this end. Every activity rightly perceived leads to this frontier.

The power which creates the potential for this growth and freedom causes genuine Christianity always to be controversial. Jesus' actions and stories – like the one about the Samaritan – linger on in the mind, disturbing and forming questions. Does one want to begin to be this new? Does one believe such an attitude is even possible for human beings? Can an individual so risk his definition of his own limitations? In and through the parables of and about him Jesus stands forward as an incitement to such risk, challenging, unnerving – making some men bold, others timid when they thought themselves brave, and some angry. Perhaps each individual can experience all these emotions within himself.

It is belief in this power which also causes a faithful Christianity to be controversial in society. Possessed by this intuition of the goal towards which persons are to develop, it can be nothing other. It must continually be in some measure of conflict with any definition of mankind which for its own purposes sets limits on the value of human beings (or of some human beings), whether this definition be philosophical, economic or political in character. Although Christians may be in dialogue with proponents of such understandings and may and in many cases should cooperate with them for the common good, this essential attitude of controversy forces committed Christian belief and practice into a truly radical stance. In the basic sense of the word *radix* the Christian witness requires the raising of questions which go to the *root* of fundamental issues involving human values. The questions themselves touch upon every manner of individual and corporate concern: the use of men and money for military purposes, employment policies, welfare programmes, abortion, medical transplants, amnesty, the use of environmental resources, and so forth. The primary concern, however, is not that Christians must agree on all these issues, but that they should be able to discuss and involve themselves with them from the radical perspective of men and women who share a fundamental agreement about their significance. In an important sense such discussions are to be conducted in the *imitation of Christ* who through a number of controversial incidents in the gospels showed himself concerned, not to deliver specific answers to questions that were asked of him involving matters like divorce, taxation and justice in religious and political affairs, but to cause his questioners to reflect radically upon the nature and purpose of human sexuality, society and personal relations.

It would seem to have been part of his purpose to bring his contemporaries out from behind their labels as Pharisees or Sadducees, opponents or supporters of the governing authorities, and to ask them to go beyond what they felt to be their own best economic or image-preserving interests. Again they were to venture forward in response to the hope of the kingdom's in-breaking edge. They were to be willing to risk something personal by asking *root* questions of themselves and also learning to ask them together with those with whom formerly they believed no open discourse could be meaningful or even possible. By himself reframing questions from the perspective of the boundary – where divine and human concerns might be seen to converge – and by posing startling possibilities of viewpoint by means of parabolic discourse, Jesus sought to bring fresh dimension to the modes of human caring and sharing.

If such grounds for meeting in the imitation of Christ are to be rediscovered and explored, the essential nature of their climate must also be realized. The atmosphere is not characterized merely by efforts at a spirit of human goodwill. Nor is it manufactured by the manipulation of feelings of guilt which are the strings in the hands of so many would-be reformers but which, despite initial results, end only by tying people more tightly to their anxieties and fears of openness. Instead it is recognized by its aura of new power – that sense of unmerited and unconditional forgiveness and acceptance which is of the kingdom. Here men and women meet with differing backgrounds of experience and levels of knowledge and expertise, but also with a conviction of their own and each other's absolute equality and inestimable value before God. They come together not anticipating the avoidance of all controversy – indeed expecting it if radical issues are to be raised and their own values and standards of righteousness are to be radically researched. Candour and even anger will not be missing in such dialogue, while yet there is the expectation that the rancour of distrust can be replaced by a community of mutual acceptance which feels for ways to heal wounds rather than to exacerbate them.

There is, of course, always danger in opening oneself and one's group to such *re*searching. So-called conservatives and liberals will find the real grounds for their conservatism and liberalism questioned from a perspective that is not entirely their own. Yet always it is the hope that such discourse will begin to discover points of convergence in human concern which will enable the possibility of genuine dialogue. It is of the essence of this Christian faith that only from the perspective of the boundary – where the power of unconditional acceptance and the trust so engendered and an intuition of an absolute source supporting reverence for human values are to be found – will the leverage be gained to enhance the human condition. Only with the end goals in sight may it become possible to accomplish the proximate goals, for it is the vision of the greatest purposes that generates the faith that peace and justice can be achieved by the means of justice and peace through individual acts and measures of government.

So it is this faith which is intended to give birth to the daring trust that, although sin and its evil are necessary, all things are open to revaluation. The story of the falling away of men and women from their potential for goodness and enhancement is thus reinterpreted and made into a drama with many new scenes and acts. Without coming into direct contact with the forces of evil, individuals and society could never learn of creation's greatest gift – the power to grow towards a freedom which, though costly, enables human beings to share in God's own determination to make the creation of the possibilities for both good and evil worth the risk entailed.

Viewed through the eyes of this hope it becomes possible to read the chapters of the Bible and the stories of individual lives and human history as a painful but awesome engagement. They tell of the struggles to gain the freedom to serve purposes that are at once a people's own but always greater than those of the individual parts of creation. However far they are fallen from their own potential, however much they have turned their backs on the possibility of human enhancement, however fearful they may be of the pain that freedom and growth always involve – from within these men and women God's Spirit calls them to become the pioneers of his intentions for the creation of the world.

Imprisoned in Egypt by their own fears, then cringing and complaining as they went and often longing to return to slavery's irresponsibilities, the people of Israel were led out of the house of bondage by a Spirit greater than their own. As was their ancestor Abraham before them, they were called to a mysterious and un-certain future. They were made to be a pilgrim people with their only security the promise of God that he would lead them through trial and struggle to a new potentiality for their humanity.

Above all it was a question of freedom of worship. In giving up all other security to decide for this freedom they were choosing God and his kingdom. Israel was electing to worship only that which they believed to have true and lasting value. All else had to be surrendered for the sake of that venture in the direction of a trust relationship with the Lord above all gods who alone was the source and goal of their liberty.

The call was to stand up and to recognize that the chains of hopelessness and fear could be broken open by the hammer of courage on the anvil of faith. The only real sin would be to turn back or to wish to camp and wait for death's peace in the wilderness – to surrender to the faithlessness that they and mankind had no destiny and that the future did not belong to God. Yet always there were forged new experiences in history which shattered the delimiting securities they strove to build for themselves and always there was the promise calling them to the frontier of possibility. God had chosen them to be scouts in the immense journey of his creative dream.

They were lured out of the garden of innocence by a capability to choose a direction which led away from their potential in relationship to the goals of existence – a necessary risk which the source of all life had countenanced and for which he took the ultimate responsibility. Their forefathers were continually being called to make for themselves new lives. In the midst of slavery to forces they seemed powerless to control, and then from an exile and alienation which their estrangement from God's purposes had brought upon them, they were beckoned and cajoled to dream anew. Jesus' message and ministry were again a challenge to come forward – to trust that the domination of evil and sickness could be overcome and to have faith that men and women could have a relationship with that which gave meaning to all life. The new relationship was to be found not in the safety of seeking to avoid acts of sin in negative terms but in a bold, almost reckless abandon in trust to the power of accepting love in all human situations.

Through subsequent history individuals and societies have experienced similar disenfranchisements from the houses of security they so vainly seek to build for themselves. Jesus' story of the man who sat back contentedly with his plans for full granaries completed only suddenly to face his death is paradigmatic for the real circumstances of life which all must learn. Fear of the changes and chances of life understandably causes all peoples to wish to build and hide behind such securities, but sooner or later they are always seen to be façades. In our own day environmental crises, food and energy shortages and the demands of swelling numbers of poor people and nations remind once more how thin the façade remains even for the most powerful and wealthy. In highly biblical terms little Middle Eastern states – so long looked down upon by the great developed nations – suddenly are seen to possess a stranglehold on the growth rates upon which the security of great nations' economies are based. Technology, with its power to destroy environmental balance and to enable warfare of incalculable proportions, becomes an awesome threat to the very security it seemed to guarantee.

Such dramatic ironies and reversals in fortune are frequently interpreted in the Bible as evidence in support of the consistent witness to God's purpose of standing on the side of the weak and powerless and opposing his face to the manifold aspects of human oppression. The song of Mary in Luke's gospel lyricizes in the name of the mother of Jesus the faith of both Israel and Christianity in God's willingness to work through his Spirit for a renewing justice.

> He has shown strength with his arm,
>   he has scattered the proud in the imagination of their hearts,
> He has put down the mighty from their thrones,
>   and exalted those of low degree;
> He has filled the hungry with good things,
>   and the rich he has sent empty away.

The point is not that the God of the Old and New Testaments fights only for the liberation of the downtrodden. He is against the power of the proud and rich also for their sakes – to free them from the prison which they too must inhabit if their lives are seen to depend on the control of others. The aggrandizer needs to be liberated from his control over those from whom he profits as much as they need their bondage broken to begin to value their own human potential. Into the hands of the people of God the Spirit seeks to give the courage and the power to dismantle the bars which society may have forged for them and to step forward as human beings – men and women free to choose to serve that which is of ultimate value in life.

5

Man and God

Still Jesus had been put to death without any sign from God. He died rejected by his own people as a dreamer and an oftentimes scandalous person. He was crucified because he was a dangerous nuisance and because he was of no value to the Pontius Pilates of the world. Surely this was the irrefutable evidence of that which men had always feared and what too much of life's experience had clubbed them into believing? The one who most trusted in God, who had offered a dream of God's loving justice, died in agony with only other criminals for whatever company one finds while dying. Though they probably are also tokens of his stubborn hope, his last words seem to indicate just how fully he was made to face the terror of death's dark and silent precipice: 'My God, my God, why have you forsaken me?'

This death must have made the disciples bury even the fragments of their hope. They had never really understood Jesus or his dream. His insistence on exposing himself to the dangers in Jerusalem and the manner of his death were incomprehensible. Though they had learned to love him almost in spite of himself, he had led what in many ways was a useless and disreputable life in the eyes of his culture. Now it had come to a shocking end. As John the Baptist had found he was forced to do before them, his followers had also to ask how he could be the Expected One? It had seemed as though he might be – that he was beginning to fulfil the aspirations of the new age of which the scriptures had spoken. Yet in retrospect, he had also acted in so many unexpected ways. His utter rejection by the leaders of Judaism and his wretched and powerless death were the final and devastating blows to their aspirations for him.

As in his life, so in his death, he had left far more questions than he had begun to answer. The most radical question of all was poignantly raised and seemingly answered with unmistakable silence by his passion and crucifixion. Can God and his relationship with his creation be trusted?

What was difficult for them to understand was why they felt impelled to go on asking the question. Was it but a forlorn need of human beings to have some kind of hope with which to live that made them whisper into the silence? Yes, they had known experiences with him that made it seem possible. They had felt with him a mysterious apprehension that a new power for life could work through their words and actions. Yet maybe that was all but a trick of his personality, a rare gift that had gone to the grave with his dream. Now the only remnant they had left was his crazy and stubborn habit of singing against the darkness.

But the strangest thing of all: the tune seemed still to have a kind of beauty and strength to it. Why, in spite of everything, did they sense a resonance, the timbre of chords? Not only was he still provoking them to ask the question, it was as though he was yet evoking a response. He had persisted in trusting to the end. His trust was somehow beginning to ameliorate their hurt, to heal their distrust. Could one go on beyond the end, through the crucifixion? Was it conceivable that the cross was God's way of sharing in the pain and evil of the world – of enduring – of insisting that it was nevertheless worthwhile to live and to love, and so beginning to reshape, causing the shameful cross to appear differently?

Just among themselves they began to tell his stories again, to recount what he had done and the activities they had shared with him. They tried to take up the stance he had helped them to present towards life, to think once more about the possibility of living on that frontier where the power of God's coming kingdom interacted with life's realities. They shared meals and remembered.

And as they did these things together – as they faced in the direction he had pointed out to them and once more felt themselves wanting to hope for the possibility of God's presence there – they became aware again of a sense of being heard and of unaccountable trust and power tugging at the edges of their experience. At this boundary God's Spirit seemed still to be moving towards them.

Far more unaccountably, this Spirit seemed now to be known to them: Yes, from beyond their experience and understanding, but also echoing, familiar, personal. It was resonate, reminding of Jesus' words and the sacrament that his voice had become to them. It was calling them out to new trust as he had done, supporting and challenging them.

They found themselves wanting to tell the stories to others, to act as he had taught them to act. Had he not told them that life's meaning could include death? Had he not said that God's power was stronger than death, that his righteous and caring justice would not be defeated?

Was he not now causing them to express the belief that they were not left as orphans in an uncaring world? Yes, he: Jesus! They were not alone when they trusted and spoke like this. When they shared their meals they were more than remembering. Strange and enrapturing encounters began to compel a faith that he could still reach through the mode of human encounter personally to touch their lives. At first haltingly, not knowing what language might be used, they began to speak of this. The conviction became so intense; it was as though at times he was personally present.

The fascination was with a sense of person who met his disciples unexpectedly and called them forward from anything which might be characterized as a ghetto of past-oriented religious experience. At the same time when, in their bewildered terror after the crucifixion, Jesus' friends dared to orient themselves in hope again towards the possibility of trusting in God, the experience of God's presence they now had reminded them of experiences they had shared with Jesus. So much was this their impression that their prayers reveal a seeming carelessness in speaking of the Spirit of God and the Spirit of Jesus interchangeably. But such is a carelessness which reflects this experience of looking towards

God and finding their association with Jesus recreated and alive.

The resolution of this echoing between experience and reminiscence is presented by the several gospels in their different ways. The memories concerning Jesus are given new value and are reinterpreted in their telling because they are stories of and about one who is perceived in direct relationship with the Lord God. Moreover, this Spirit of Jesus does not remain silent, but through prayer and prophecy speaks new words which help to interpret those already known. In the preaching and teaching of the communities of Christians these sayings mingle and are recognized as the words of and about the one Jesus. The once-known person and his new form of presence are viewed as through a stereoscope. The two images contribute depth and meaning's colour to form a single picture of the Lord Jesus. The acceptance, challenge and forgiveness realized in the Spirit are seen as congruent with and regenerative of experiences which the disciples had known with Jesus. The style and stance towards life to which Jesus had called them is remembered in association with the renewing Spirit. Each set of experiences now contained clues for the interpretation of the other.

Now it was more fully understood that Jesus had not only spoken the words of God; he had enacted them. He had not only told parables, but he had done them – standing in and behind his words. He had spoken with an authority surpassing that of other teachers because of the integrity between his words and deeds. He did not just say that those regarded as sinners were recognized by God as his own. He forgave their sins and accepted them. In what seemed near blasphemy to the religious establishment (and no doubt to many who were trying to follow him as well), Jesus was found among the people regarded as of no account, forgiving them in God's name and associating himself with them.

Given many of men's usual religious preoccupations, it is extraordinary that the gospels place their stress upon such actions of Jesus and have so little to say about the things he did *not* do. His sinlessness is not presented in negative terms. This sometimes proves a source of embarrassment to those who would like to make Jesus an exemplar for their own particular emphasis on that which involves not sinning.

What instead imprinted itself upon the approach to life by his disciples and so is best remembered in and for the life of the Christian community was Jesus' positive concern for others. He sought out opportunities to accept and forgive people like Zacchaeus, giving them the dignity and space to hope again and to grow as human beings. Other stories like the healings on the sabbath and the woman forgiven her adultery indicate a freedom to reach beyond the limited view of the potential for human caring on which the law's understanding of necessity was based. So surprising were these activities and his own unconcern with the self-protective roles provided by human customs that it was difficult for both friend and foe alike to find any convenient pattern to which he might be conformed. As is true of each human being who finds him or herself entrammelled in the sins and prejudices of society, so Jesus could not wholly escape the limitations which were part of his social structure. Yet he seems always to have been exploring beyond them – unwilling to set any limit for caring. One may believe that it was this extraordinary liberty more than anything else which provoked the fear and jealousy which led to his crucifixion.

So remembered in their own lives by his followers Jesus had done far more than to speak of a new possibility of relationship between men and with God. He had brought it to living expression. He was in person the bearer of God's word – the human statement of God's acceptance and forgiveness and a challenge pointing the way towards that which men and women might become. No longer was it the preaching about the divine kingdom which formed the heart of the burgeoning faith. Rather was the awareness growing that the new possibility of relationship had broken through the boundary between humanity and the transcendent in Jesus himself. As one early church teacher was to state it, Jesus was *autobasileia*, that is, the kingdom's embodiment. The retelling of his life, death and new life became the consummate parable of the new faith.

So do the narratives and sayings of and about him become the chief community-forming stories for the disciples. They are treasured as the code experiences which, when faithfully retold and heard, guide in the interpretation of new incidents believed to begin to reveal truths of an ultimate character. The manner in which such re-enactment can become recreative revelation is best appreciated by many Christians in the Last Supper or Holy Communion: 'Do this in remembrance of me.'

As it remains difficult for us to find the ideas and language which will convey some sense of how a man's life and words might come to be so valued, we can imagine the early disciples searching in their minds and hearts for the words to help themselves and others interpret their experiences of him. Jesus himself had been of little help. Several incidents in the gospels illustrate a seemingly deliberate intention on his part to deflect any categorizing attempts at understanding. Careful research indicates that Jesus probably never replied with any other than a studied ambiguity to efforts to define his ministry in terms of a title or office. What answers he gave point beyond himself to the frontier which can only be explored as a venture of faith. One may surmise that who he was remained a kind of mystery to him. He, too, was still experiencing and discovering God's intentions and thus could and would not make absolute claims for himself. He could only act as herald for the new possibility which was in the world and seemed powerful in his ministry. In faith men had to make up their own minds about how they would respond to his message and to him.

Although, even after the resurrection, the disciples must have recognized that Jesus' meaning for them could never be comprehended by the shorthand of titles and designations of dignity, it was inevitable that they would grasp at such verbal handles in their efforts to say something regarding their perception of who Jesus was and is. He was certainly a teacher and rabbi, one who could interpret the law with unsurpassed authority and whose words bore the heritage of the ancient wisdom tradition. He was a prophet, perhaps even *the* prophet like Moses or Elijah who, it was predicted, would return before the close of the ages. Perhaps in conjunction with special forms of this prophetic expectation, he was regarded in some quarters as the Son of Man, a heavenly judge who might also be thought to have a representative or counterpart on earth. Or he was the especially chosen of the Lord, the anointed one, the Messiah (in Greek, the Christ).

At the same time, however, the preaching and teaching disciples were faced with the task of explaining how this Expected One could have behaved in such unexpected ways and especially how it was that God's Messiah should have been condemned by the Roman authorities and have died ignominious and powerless by means of crucifixion. As Paul expressed it, 'we preach Christ crucified, a stumbling block to Jews and folly to the Gentiles'. Both Jew and Gentile doubtless wondered, as have others since that time, if the cross was not evidence that Jesus was at the least a misguided visionary or perhaps an advocate of political revolution whose death, though possibly tragic, was like that of many others before him whose ideas and actions displeased the powers of society. When the genuine representative of God came, he would not present himself in weakness, but in glory and in the power of God's own strength.

Such were the odds that the early Christians found themselves facing. Searching the scriptures for guidance, they fastened upon the figure of the *servant* of the Lord from the book of the prophet Isaiah as being predictive of the one who would be 'despised and rejected by men, a man of sorrows and acquainted with grief . . . through whose wounds we are healed'. This, however, was far from a completely satisfactory explanation of his condemnation as a criminal. The disciples' persistence derived, not from any full understanding of why this should have been so, but from their experience of the man who had shared with them new insights into God's ways of relating to his creatures and who, they believed, had been raised from the dead. These were personal ways which included lowliness and the acceptance of pain and evil before triumph over them could be achieved. They had entered into the mystery of fellowship with a human being whom they believed to have been and to be the means by which divine life betokened his affinity with his suffering creation.

Yes, Jesus was a teacher and the hoped-for prophet. He was the Son of Man and the promised Messiah who was also God's servant. Yet all of these titles – even when taken together – did not seem to say enough. They were not sufficiently descriptive and, in some cases, had too little coinage in the areas outside Palestine in which the stories about Jesus were now beginning to be told. The designations retained their place in the traditions, but the realization grew that the person could not be contained within the definitions of such offices or titles. Moreover, it became more important to try to indicate that the whole idea of Messiahship or Christhood had been fulfilled in Jesus than simply to make the confession 'Jesus is the Christ'. The title belonged to him and not he to it. For many later generations of Christians it must have seemed as though the title had become his last name: he was Jesus Christ. The awareness grew that the manner in which God had expressed himself was pre-eminently personal in character. A sense of God's presence was recognized through and in his person, and thus the most important name became his 'name which is above every name, that at the name of Jesus every knee should bow'.

And with this experience of so worshipping Jesus there grew stronger the realization that he might also be spoken of as *Lord*. Even though it was to cause misunderstanding and later the enmity of persecution on the part of those who reserved the title Lord for Caesar and so gave their highest allegiance to the state – and, though it meant controversy with many who held to the orthodoxy of their Jewish heritage, Christians felt themselves impelled by the Holy Spirit to praise and sing of Jesus with the same invocation that Judaism otherwise reserved for God himself. In a number of their hymns and acclamations it becomes difficult to ascertain whether it is God or Jesus who is being addressed. Such imprecision was, however, the fruit of the experience of finding oneself praying 'through Jesus Christ our Lord' when seeking to be *towards* God in one's life. Those men and women, who were at first derogatorily called Christians, came to accept this name as their own and painfully to separate themselves and to be separated from the religion of their fathers. Judaism's promise, they believed, had begun to be fulfilled in a way which did not destroy but forced them well beyond the structures of Judaism.

The proclamation that Jesus is Lord also meant to those coming from other faiths that Jesus was to be understood as the fulfilment of their religious aspirations. There could be no other lords beside him. This was an era of great religiosity in the Mediterranean world. In addition to the older religions and philosophies there had been an influx of new faiths from Egypt and the Near East. Cultic saviour figures were presented as having the powers, through special initiatory rites and rituals, to save their adherents from death and the world's travails. For many it was a time of cultural pessimism in which the created universe had come to be viewed as a sphere of error and decay inimical to human life and human values. Men were powerless to change their fortune unless aided by secret knowledge given to them from a distant realm that was distinct from the evil creation. The divine spark in men would be rescued out of the world by means of this saving knowledge. Now, however, Jesus was seen as a world and life-affirming saviour whose triumph over death, men's cruelty and the restrictions of human futility offered a new way to perceive the world and to fulfil the dreams of a relationship with God. Though it would lead them away from an easy syncretism and towards further controversy in their societies, those who held Jesus to be the Lord had to worship him as representative of the God of all life and all creation. He was greater than any of the fatalistic astral deities or other gods who stood distant from the world. He was the only true Lord. Only he was worthy of worship because he alone could enable men to believe that all life's experience was redeemable.

The manner in which this faith in Jesus was growing from earlier roots in the disciples' experience can be further illustrated from the use of another title which also had status, although with different estimations, in both Judaism and the Hellenistic world. We can imagine that the term *son of God* might first have been applied to Jesus as it would have been to any Jew who was regarded as faithful to the will of God understood as father-like. The sense of this usage is found in Jesus' own words when he tells his followers that they must love their enemies . . . 'and you will be sons of the Most High'. Those who are God's sons emulate the character of the Father who is righteous, forgiving and merciful. To his followers Jesus himself had clearly been such a son of God.

Not for long, however, were the disciples able to leave the evaluation of Jesus at this level of meaning. They, of course, were only groping towards understanding but, at the very least, it was a matter of degree. Jesus' reflection of God's will had seemed to them far truer than that of other good men. The depth of his faithfulness and of his obedience even to the point of death were of a character to set him apart, and the vindication and affirmation of the resurrection signified a very special kind of relationship.

In reminiscence the disciples recalled his sense of intimacy with the God whom he called Father, coupled with an authority to forgive and accept others in this Father-God's name which they had witnessed in association with Jesus. It was not that he had been willing to advertise himself as God's son, but rather the way he had spoken in familiar terms of God as Father, that they remembered. The gospels preserve recollections indicating that Jesus had done this in a manner which surprised and may even have scandalized. What appears to be the most primitive version of the Lord's Prayer began simply, 'Father'. The original form of this direct way of speaking of God is very likely preserved in the Aramaic word reported to have been used by Jesus and also, according to Paul, carried forward in the prayer language of the early Christian communities. Jesus was remembered as having spoken to and of God as *Abba*. While this address is not unknown in Jewish prayers, Jesus seems to have given it a particular intensity as is also suggested by his use of the analogy of God's fatherhood in a number of his sayings and stories. To gain something of the flavour of the word we need to recall for a moment how it is that a baby learns to talk. The most natural sound is the relaxed and open-throated *aaahh*. One day the infant accidentally closes his lips and the sound comes out as *maah-maah*. Instantly over the cradle there appears the delighted and smiling maternal face. The baby is picked up and cuddled. With such reinforcement the child gradually learns to make the sound voluntarily.

On another occasion the tongue comes into play and the sound is heard as *daah-daah*. A different beaming face appears, and the reinforcement of another word begins. In the Aramaic language a similar process would have taken place as the lips easily and naturally created the sound *aabbah*. The word *Abba* was, therefore, bound to retain in the ears of its hearers the resonance of a child's intimate relationship with his father. Jesus' use of the expression, when coupled with his striking analogies descriptive of the fatherhood of God, clearly left an indelible impression on his disciples.

From such reminiscences, and through their resurrection faith, the conviction grew in Jesus' followers that God was his Father in a special sense. Jesus had in an unexampled way lived as his son, reflecting in human life the will and character of this Father-God. He came to be spoken of as *the* Son of God.

This understanding of Jesus was amplified in the gospel according to John. Jesus in human person so well represented the character of God that he could be presented as saying, 'He who has seen me has seen the Father.' The stress was not only on the functional way that Jesus had acted as the Son of God, but there began to develop a concern to show that he was a manifestation of God's very nature. Moreover, if Jesus was to be understood as a genuine revelation of God, there must be a sense in which the aspect of the divinity which was his had always been existent. While those who had made earlier attempts to interpret Jesus' relationship with God were probably content to believe that his human person had been chosen and adopted by God to become his Son, now the fourth evangelist maintained that that which was godly in him must always have been so. What other of the gospels had begun to allude to by means of nature miracles and birth narratives, this evangelist stated more directly.

> When all things began, the Word already was. The Word dwelt with God, and what God was, the Word was. The Word, then, was with God at the beginning, and through him all things came to be; no single thing was created without him. All that came to be was alive with his life.

The divinity which was expressed in and through Jesus' person must always have been of God in order to be divine. This was none other than the creative power through which the whole universe had been given its existence, and which now had been glimpsed by Jesus' followers through the prism of one human life. 'No one has ever seen God; but God's only Son, he who is nearest to the Father's heart, he has made him known.'

Belief in this relationship could become so intensified in the faith perception of his followers as to cause them to say on Jesus' behalf, 'I and the Father are one.' Yet it is important to remain aware that the unity so realized still is understood as rooted in the analogy of affinity between a son and a father. It is a kinship based on filial obedience and mutuality of wills. Human attempts to give statement to the association in terms of metaphysical language continue secondary to the understanding of a relationship based on ethical agreement. Jesus is the Son of God because he has in person made available a human translation of the character of God's love. In a forcefully repetitive manner the closing discourses of the fourth gospel press home the belief that the Son can be said to indwell the Father and the Father the Son because of their love for one another and their mutual love for the disciples. Into the mystery of this association the disciples, through their response of love, are invited to enter. Only here do they begin to perceive that Jesus, to have been and to be the human catalyst for this relationship, must have been now and always of God–that the divine character which he presented needs to be recognized as eternal in its significance and transcendental in its origin. The light which he had caused to shine in their hearts was not merely the reflected light as of a satellite. The light had issued from the depths of his own being.

It was left to later generations of Christians to probe this faith fired in the kiln of the worshipping of Jesus. How could a being be regarded as a human person and yet so of God as to be worshipped as God? In some sense, of course, the problem can have no answer from a mortal point of view. Human beings have a difficult enough time understanding their own species. A divine nature which transcends direct human experience and the manner in which such divinity could relate to their reality are beyond any possibility of full comprehension. Yet it is also impossible for men to own such a faith and not attempt at least to make approaches in the direction of trying to understand.

The ventures towards explanation have been various and rooted in different views of reality in given cultures and generations. A number of the more notable efforts involved attempts to conceive of Jesus as a kind of hybrid being. It was held that Jesus was human in terms of body and basic emotions but divine in his mental capacities. When it was recognized that there was no realistic way in which such a being could be said to share fully in the human condition, the argument then was put forward that, while he was human in body and mind, Jesus' highest spiritual faculties, including his own awareness of his relationship to God, were divine. Again this was perceived to be an insufficient understanding of what it really meant to be a human being. If Jesus so differed from other men – if there was some aspect of him that did not participate fully in all that human life entails – then at heart it became impossible for others to identify with him in his daily experiences and especially in his suffering and death.

On the other hand, those who wished so to stress Jesus' humanity as to exclude the possibility that divine Being could have in some manner shared directly in his human life also were seen to have missed an equally essential truth. The concern of such early theologians was often that of preserving the complete transcendence and total otherness of God. God, they believed, could not in any way be said to have suffered in Jesus. Such was their understanding of God that he otherwise could not be regarded as a perfect and unchanging Being. The most they would grant was that he had associated himself sympathetically with Jesus' experiences, but had always maintained the necessary distinctions between the divine and human orders of existence.

Yet, if divine Being had not in some more authentic fashion allowed himself to participate in all that it means to be human, how could it be maintained that he had really given of himself in the life of Jesus? Empathetic association was not enough and, beyond this, men could not worship as their Lord one who was only human, however good. Yet the experience of Christians was that Jesus was not just to be admired – not merely reverenced – but worshipped as signifying and manifesting forth that which was of ultimate worth and meaning.

Thus, however difficult it might be to formulate in theological language or in terms of the logic of men's understanding of the natures of humanity and divinity, the practical experience of worshipping and praying Christians won out and was finally incorporated into doctrinal statements. Jesus was fully and completely human, one with whom other men and women could wholly identify. This humanity continued to be his after his resurrection and remained as the bridge between human and divine reality. Yet he was genuinely of God as well, being God's articulation of himself in the world – his Word, bringing to expression in the language of a human life the possibilities that are of his creative nature. The passion and death of Jesus were not a sacrifice required of an individual by a transcendent Being, but God's way of sharing and giving of himself in his creation.

Statements of Christian faith, codified in conciliar formulas and creeds, cannot, however, be regarded as solutions to the theological questions arising from the experience of Jesus as Lord. At best they are simplified attempts within the limits of language and a particular culture's understanding to give expression to the vital issues found to be involved. More contemporary efforts in the direction of understanding recognize the necessity for framing questions concerning the manner in which men think and talk about God and about what a human person is. Such discussion also raises the issue of the relationship that might be believed to exist between human and divine life.

Among the more useful *models* or ways of reflecting on the possibility of God today are those which seek to avoid difficulties felt by many modern individuals when attempting to conceive of God as though another Being apart from or alongside the universe. The emphasis falls instead upon a sense of his presence which is to be known from the inside and not, as it were, from the outside of creation. He is not best apprehended in the gaps in our understanding nor in terms of occasional intrusions into our reality from beyond it. Rather is his creative activity (which Jesus' sayings and stories speak of as the kingdom of God) to be perceived in and amid the very processes of life.

Though to some such understandings may seem like a new way of thinking about God, they are actually similar to several of the oldest faith conceptions in the world. Many earlier men described through their religions a sense of divine reality permeating all that is – bringing the gift of existence to all things. Such models represent a way of maintaining that existence is in a contiguous – even intimate – relationship with its ultimate basis of being. They seek to express a hope or belief that, despite apparent contradictions, there is a perspective from which all reality is not in final contradiction – that there is a unifying wholeness. The Bible makes use of such language when it speaks of God as the one in whom 'we live, and move, and have our being'. Related perceptions of God are certainly to be found in Eastern religions and are present to a remarkable extent in the writings of mystics of many faiths. God is immanent in the world of human realities, vitally and essentially of it in such a manner that in no way can he be described as another Being apart from it. His transcendence of this world is best understood not with an emphasis on apartness, but as his being that upon which all things are dependent in order to be.

Many other philosophical and theological questions are, of course, raised by these thoughts. One recognizes that all such language is used only by way of analogy, a method with built-in inadequacies because analogies suggest both more and less than one wishes to say. Yet a great advantage of these approaches to reflection lies in their power to help people contemplate how God might be experienced at the same time as hidden and yet not absent from their lives. Such a God cannot be known or comprehended as we would attempt to be aware of things or beings which are other from us. He is not to us some force or power wholly separate from us in our world. We cannot stand apart and observe him because we too are of him in order that we may have our existence.

This way of thinking would suggest that all things that exist are manifestations of God, but these expressions are understood to be of different orders. Though it might be regarded as but a result of the limitations of our understanding, the human capacity for self-consciousness and awareness does seem to give to mankind a special status in the known creation. It is not merely that man thinks. Such might be said, to one degree or another, of other creatures. What appears to set human beings distinctly apart is their ability to be aware that they are thinking – to reflect upon their own thoughts and to be in dialogue with themselves. It might be said that, when certain of our ancestors first attained and realized this capability, at that moment human life was begun.

Here for the first time individuality and personhood became an actuality and so also the relationship of individuals as a society became possible. As an essential part of the same phenomenon the capacity for true language was born, and men began to shape their reality through words. If we stand back and attempt to look at this phenomenon through fresh sight, we may gain some sense of amazement that such consciousness should ever have arisen.

Probably ever since consciousness began men and women have in one way or another asked themselves the question whether this awareness might be a singular and otherwise companionless phenomenon in the universe. Excepting the perhaps never to be known possibility that there is conscious life on other planetary systems, men wonder whether their self-awareness is but an isolated product of the variations of evolutionary processes. Does it exist in lonely distinction from all other matter and forms of life in a universe otherwise dark to the lamp of consciousness?

The questioning has never received a univocal or even generally accepted response. Even to ask whether the human consciousness may have some form of companionship produces a kind of existential dread in most hearts for fear the answer might be an eternal *no*, condemning this species in its self-awareness to be but a lonely aberration without other relationship in the forever silent universe. In such circumstances the dangers involved in answering the question in the affirmative, merely to escape the burden of loneliness, are obvious. Nonetheless, there must be taken into account the fact that hosts of men and women, some acutely aware of the dangers of self-deception, have believed that their self-awareness can have a relationship with a form of self-awareness which is fundamental to their entire being. In religious terms this capacity for human beings to engage in dialogue with and in some sense transcend themselves in awareness of self has been called their spirits. The human spirit is then believed to be capable of the possibility of relationship with an analogous aware-ness – or Spirit – of God. For many religious people it is this Spirit – this divine consciousness – which they perceive to be the source of and the context for their own capacity for consciousness and self-awareness.

If asked how one might have a sense of God's presence, a

believer can respond in terms of the opportunity to explore all the capabilities of his spirit – to become truly present to himself. At the heights and depths of his personal being he seeks to discover a creative expressiveness which gives life and offers dialogue to conscious existence. There also is the opportunity to know others as fully as one can share in their humanity and so to enter in some measure into their sense of participation in ultimate reality. This perception of God giving life to others, especially in the lives of those who are different from oneself and hold variant values, is one of the greatest safeguards against mere idolatry and mistaking what is only of oneself for God. In biblical language such understandings are presented when human beings are said to exist in the image of God. The New Testament insists that men and women can claim neither to know nor love God unless they love the beings created in his image, for so God is made known in the world.

With these thoughts in mind we may return to the question as to how contemporary disciples might speak of Jesus. In our terms we may conclude that the first Christians were maintaining that Jesus was a pre-eminent manifestation in human life of God's expression of himself. This expression is made in some measure in every human life, but his disciples glimpsed more fully than in any other the possibility of Holy Being signalling and articulating himself in the activities and words of Jesus' person. He became for them a kind of aperture through which insights into the divine presence best could be perceived. Jesus is recognized as a setting forth in time of the eternal willingness of God to share of himself – to 'empty himself' forever in order that he might give of himself to mankind.

More than this, Jesus had awakened in his disciples a keener awareness of their own participation in Holy Being. He was – again in New Testament language – a *forerunner* or *pioneer* of God's intentions for human persons. In him human evolution had, as it were, taken a quantum jump – not in physical or mental capabilities – but in the ability to live by the creative power of God. In his overcoming of the inhibiting declinations towards sin and lack of personal growth, he had given his followers a clue as to the freedom for life that the positive desire to care for others – to accept and support their human potential – could accomplish. This is what the New Testament means when it speaks of the Christ that can live in his disciples and when it sets forth the goal of growing towards 'the measure of the stature of the fullness of Christ'. This astonishing idea is brought to full expression by a disciple called John: 'What we are to be in the future has not yet been revealed; all we know is that, when it is revealed, we shall be like him.' Jesus had caused his followers to realize that there are no certain limits on what persons can become because their own capabilities for creative life are rooted in the infinite personhood of All Holy Being.

The resurrection so becomes both sign and symbol that – other evidence to the contrary, entropy and death need not be the final chapters in the story of personal and social development. At the same time the mysterious character of so many of Jesus' resurrection appearances – seemingly disguised in the lives of other human beings – provokes the disciples towards the demanding and sometimes startling understanding that it is the same personal gift of God's creativity which is seeking to manifest itself in themselves and other persons. 'As you did it to one of the least of these my brethren,' announces Jesus, 'you did it to me.'

The disciples are thus again confronted with the awareness that – however much they might think they would wish it to be some other way – the response to God's expression of love in Jesus is to be offered in love towards others. By accepting God's care and forgiveness one comes to know oneself as lovable and so able to love others. In so loving others one finds that it is also the God seeking to come to expression in human beings that is being loved. The unifying circle formed by the two chief commandments so becomes evident. It is another way of saying what the risen Lord elsewhere expresses as one commandment: 'Love one another; just as I have loved you, you also are to love one another.' This ideal of mutuality and corporate sharing with one another is also given statement in the theme of being raised up to begin to form a new humanity with Jesus and also of the Christ who creates new community – a new body – through the participation and fellowship of the communion meal. The motif of communal concern and caring for *one another* then resonates through the New Testa-ment and is intended to echo in the different persons of the disciples as they seek to let the Spirit of Jesus be manifested in their own lives. 'Wash one another's feet'; 'forbear and forgive one another'; 'comfort one another and build each other up'; 'greet one another with the kiss of peace'; 'serve one another'; 'teach and admonish one another'; 'bear one another's burdens'; 'be at peace one with another'; 'God himself lives in us if we love one another'.

Just as unexpectedly as in his earthly life does Jesus' Spirit lead his disciples forward to discover this 'one another' in every kind of person: in the prisoner and the leper, the Samaritan, the Jew and the Gentile, women and men, slave and free. All are called and enabled to be participants in the new humanity.

Yet then again we experience uncaringness and pain in our own lives. Once more – in the face of our efforts to articulate our hopes – we are made to see how small and weak the beginning of the kingdom appears. Our fears reawaken an anxiety which tempts cynicism. There is an aspect of each one of us which, together with those first onlookers, stands watching Jesus being crucified and taunts, 'If you are the Son of God, come down from the cross.' But he will not. What kind of God is this? Why does he not change his world so that evil and agony are not part of every life – even his own?

By the standards of worldly wisdom the power of the cross is no power at all. What are forgiveness and acceptance when stood up against the other forces experienced in life? Are there really any values to which human beings may aspire which can enable them to step beyond the enslavement of being either victims or victimizers in this world? Can a gift of reconciling love break the chains of past wrong which seem not only severely to limit the possibilities for human development but even to direct processes of dehumanization? The evidence in this striped and mottled world seems so thin and inconclusive.

Thus the melody by which one walks is as mysterious as it is haunting. At times it grows indistinct, and all these questions flood back. Might not the human capacity for self-awareness be but an accident of random processes in the universe, but fragilely and perhaps only temporarily supported by a coincidence of forces themselves wholly unrelated to conscious activity? Looking out from a ridiculously small point of vantage on an inexplicable vastness – in which so much seems empty coldness pockmarked by blazes of thermo-nuclear intensity – would it not seem more logical to conclude that the universe is at best indifferent to and perhaps inimical to what we know as the human experiment? However much we long for relationship with some other form of psychic life and at times think we have found an inkling of response, does not the evidence weigh heavily in favour of our utter loneliness? Should not this dream of a heavenly Father now be discarded – having been explained as a projection out into the skies of our picture of a perfect parent which we thought we knew in our infancy but then lost in reality's experience?

It seems probable that such requestioning is unavoidable to those deeply engaged in some manner of religious quest. It is heard in the complaining voice of the psalmist, through the bleak and agonized descriptions of St John's dark night of the soul and the unknown mystical writer's *Cloud of Unknowing*, right up to the present day cries of despair and abandonment. No age has a monopoly on such thoughts of dread and loneliness, though, as we are children of the twentieth century, the results of the insensate slaughter of great wars and horrifying holocaust have inevitably affected the picture of a caring and powerful God for us all.

I remember having the feeling accidentally, though somehow tellingly, fixed for myself several years ago while teaching at an English theological college. There we practised with fair intensity the Christian forms of prayer and worship. Regularly each morning we engaged in the Anglican Morning Prayer service, followed by the Eucharist and then a period of personal reflection and meditation.

In the service of Morning Prayer, after readings from the Bible interspersed with canticles, there follows a corporate recitation of the Apostles' Creed. The leader of the service begins with the familiar words, 'I believe in God,' and then the rest of the congregation joins in the Creed's repetition. It was, however, our custom on Wednesdays and Fridays during Lent to break off from the regular Morning Prayer order just before the Creed and instead turn to the prayers and responses known as the Litany.

It must, then, have been some early Wednesday or Friday morning in that frequently chilly chapel that a sleepy student leading the service forgot the special order and instead carried on uniformly with the words, 'I believe in God.' One would perhaps have to be an Anglican worshipper to appreciate the awkwardness – the quality of embarrassment – in the silence with which this declaration was met. The huddled seminarians, knowing all too well that the special order had not been adhered to, at first averted their eyes and then began to sneak glances at one another wondering what would happen next. How were we to proceed? Then from the stall of the Principal of the College came a gentle but firm voice in a stage whisper which carried through the cold and silent chapel, 'Not on Wednesdays and Fridays.'

So for an hour or for a day or longer all seems again impossible – love's song silenced by the mighty power of evil and death. Yet then slowly, haltingly, incredibly, the rhythm begins to take shape again. The wounded healer beckons in the only way that one suspects can bring us forward – not through a knowledge which we take into ourselves and own but towards the risking of love which calls us out from ourselves. For what is one to do with the other experiences, especially those which give once again the feeling of adventure into mystery and the sense of movement towards a growth in freedom? If all such experience could honestly be discounted as resulting from needs born of a desire for escape from the brute facts of human finitude, then religious faith might be set aside or at least relegated to the status of a kind of hobby. Yet there beats at the heart of such experience this sense of being lifted – of being quested after and not merely questing. There is again the leading edge of a new power for life disclosing itself as it were a gift. As Paul expresses it, there is a revelation of 'the Spirit bearing witness with our spirit' – a cognizance of self-awareness participating in and enabled to be by an awareness far greater than one's own. It is not so much a matter of knowing as of being known – not of escape, but rather of being apprehended at the level of one's highest potentialities. The future and the definition of human possibility refuse to be closed off with the limitations seemingly imposed by the chain of cause and effect seen as moving only from the past through the present. Once again the human life cannot satisfactorily be defined solely from its own perspective.

Of course all such experience remains discountable on Wednesdays and Fridays. There is no certain defence to the arguments of others and one's own doubts suggesting that it is all a kind of psychic trick – perhaps just a curious *gestalt* which from time to time is triggered into activity. Yet for some – however inexplicably they seem selected and whether they be fools or pioneers – there is a sense of movement as in a gyre. Faith and doubt are here not enemies but activities guided by a polarity which causes those who go on trusting to circle from darkness to light to darkness and back again – and perhaps to spiral – slowly to come to a new vantage.

'I form the light and create darkness: I make peace and create evil: I the Lord do all these things,' announces the prophet in the Lord's name. Maybe we think we would prefer it some other way – even to have another kind of God. But perhaps this is the only way real life can be. The prophet boldly perceives that, given this world of evil and suffering as well as the joy of living, the only God worth believing in is the God who accepts the full responsibility for all that existence seems to entail. He not only has foreseen the risk, he has accepted all its consequences. In the crucifixion of Jesus, symbolic of all other suffering in which he participates, God shares in the horror that seems a part of the consequences of causing life to be. If it is better to create conscious life – with all its potential for wrong and suffering – than that there should be no awareness at all, God will not stand aloof from his activity. Pre-eminently in Jesus, as his enacted parable, he participates in the heartbreak of it, and by an act of compassion (of 'suffering with') accepts it as his.

In one sense the cross epitomizes the worst of human evil in action towards the fellow beings in whom God also lives and suffers. The forgiving and accepting words from that tree of death act to reconcile human beings to God and to offer them a new beginning in relationship. In another sense the cross is God's way of reconciling himself to men – of saying that this is the only way it can be and then acting through love towards the resolution of the creation's seeming contradictions. *There must be evil and pain, and I, your God, participate in it personally with you. Only by sharing it, by accepting it as necessary to the act of giving life, can we begin to transform it – to redeem it by giving it new value.* All creative love involves the possibility of being injured and hurt to the point of death. But in so offering ourselves, we may use even this as a way of growth towards new life and meaning. Only so may there be Easter and the resurrection of the purpose of life. Such faith comes to audacious expression in the vision of Julian of Norwich: 'Sin is necessary, but all will be well, all will be well; all manner of things will be well.'

Though more remains unknown than known, Christians look upon Jesus as God's personal means of reconciling himself to mankind and for all people to become forgiven for what they do to one another and to God in them. 'All this is from God, who through Christ reconciled us to himself, and . . . in Christ God was reconciling the world to himself.' Through God acting in Jesus' life, death and renewed life, a new way of relationship between God and men is made possible. Through and because of him – despite sin and the evil that we are made to suffer in our existence – we are enabled to feel and carry forward his Spirit in our hearts. At the heights and depths of human experience he shares his Spirit of Jesus which – in spite of our fears and agonized doubt – prompts our lips to form the word Abba, Father, and again to trust the risk of loving, whatever the consequences may be.

In and through Jesus the possibility is perceived that one of mankind's repeated myth dreams may have become a reality. The great king himself comes to share in the life of his people. He rules not from above but among and within. He both enjoys their life and suffers with and on behalf of them, knowing the rich colour but also the seemingly unsupportable evil of their existence. Only by so understanding and so accepting can he cause them to believe that his kingdom is worth living and worth loving for, and that – sharing with them as man – he is truly their God.

116P 322